CAMBRIAN RAILWAYS GALLERY

A PICTORIAL JOURNEY THROUGH TIME

Other books by David Maidment:

Novels (Religious historical fiction)
The Child Madonna, Melrose Books, 2009
The Missing Madonna, PublishNation, 2012
The Madonna and her Sons, PublishNation, 2015

Novels (Railway fiction)
Lives on the Line, Max Books, 2013

Non-fiction (Railways)
The Toss of a Coin, PublishNation, 2014
A Privileged Journey, Pen & Sword, 2015
An Indian Summer of Steam, Pen & Sword, 2015
Great Western Eight-Coupled Heavy Freight Locomotives, Pen & Sword, 2015
Great Western Moguls and Prairies, Pen & Sword, 2016
Southern Urie and Maunsell 2-cylinder 4-6-0s, Pen & Sword, 2016
Great Western Small-Wheeled Double-Framed 4-4-0s, Pen & Sword, 2017
The Development of the German Pacific Locomotive, Pen & Sword, 2017
Great Western Large-Wheeled Double-Framed 4-4-0s, Pen & Sword, 2017
Great Western Counties, 4-4-0s, 4-4-2Ts & 4-6-0s, Pen & Sword, 2018
Southern Maunsell 4-4-0s, Pen & Sword, 2019
Southern Railway, Maunsell Moguls and Tank Locomotive Classes, Pen & Sword, 2018
Great Western Granges, Pen & Sword, 2019

Non-fiction (Street Children)
The Other Railway Children, PublishNation, 2012
Nobody ever listened to me, PublishNation, 2012

Other books by Paul Carpenter

Recreating the Night Owl – 4709- the story so far

Front Cover photo: 7823 *Hook Norton Manor* leaving Machynlleth with the Aberystwyth portion of the *Cambrian Coast Express*, c1963. (Andrew Dyke collection)

Back Cover photos:
'Dean Goods', No.2449, bringing a ballast train from the quarry in the Tanat Valley back to Blodwell Junction, Porthywaen and Oswestry, c1953. (Andrew Dyke colourisation/National Library of Wales)

'Dukedog' 9016 at Oswestry with a Whitchurch – Aberystwyth train, the former Cambrian Railways HQ in the background, 1950. (Andrew Dyke colourisation)

All royalties from this book will be donated to the Railway Children charity [reg. no. 1058991] [www.railwaychildren.org.uk]

CAMBRIAN RAILWAYS GALLERY

A PICTORIAL JOURNEY THROUGH TIME

DAVID MAIDMENT AND PAUL CARPENTER

PEN & SWORD
TRANSPORT

AN IMPRINT OF PEN & SWORD BOOKS LTD.
YORKSHIRE – PHILADELPHIA

First published in Great Britain in 2019 by
Pen and Sword Transport
An imprint of
Pen & Sword Books Ltd
Yorkshire - Philadelphia

ISBN 978 1 52673 603 1

A CIP catalogue record for this book is available from the British Library.

Typeset by Aura Technology and Software Services, India
Printed and bound in China through Printworks Global Ltd.

Pen & Sword Books Ltd incorporates the Imprints of Pen & Sword Books Archaeology, Atlas, Aviation,
Battleground, Discovery, Family History, History, Maritime, Military, Naval, Politics, Railways, Select,
Transport, True Crime, Fiction, Frontline Books, Leo Cooper, Praetorian Press, Seaforth Publishing,
Wharncliffe and White Owl.

For a complete list of Pen & Sword titles please contact

PEN & SWORD BOOKS LIMITED
47 Church Street, Barnsley, South Yorkshire, S70 2AS, England
E-mail: enquiries@pen-and-sword.co.uk
Website: www.pen-and-sword.co.uk

or

PEN AND SWORD BOOKS
1950 Lawrence Rd, Havertown, PA 19083, USA
E-mail: Uspen-and-sword@casematepublishers.com
Website: www.penandswordbooks.com

CONTENTS

ACKNOWLEDGEMENTS

There have been many books about the Cambrian Railways, but recently two collections of photographs have come to hand and the authors have been fortunate in obtaining permission of their owners to publish these in this Pen & Sword book in the 'Gallery' series of transport history. We therefore acknowledge with gratitude the Manchester Locomotive Society and their photo archivist, Paul Shackcloth, for permission to publish the locomotive and train photographs from former MLS Chairman, R.W. (Bob) Miller, who, back in 1967, wrote with a colleague, Rex Christiansen, one of the definitive two-volume histories of the Cambrian Railways. The other is a collection of magnificent photographs owned by Andrew Dyke who has also given us permission to publish a selection from his vast collection so that they may be enjoyed by all those who love the Cambrian railway lines and value their past. Andrew has enhanced a number of these using modern digital techniques by the process of 'colourisation' that renders them almost

Black liveried 7807 *Compton Manor* heads a Whitchurch – Machynlleth stopping train approaching Abermule station, 10 March 1959. (Andrew Dyke collection)

indistinguishable from modern colour photographs, and where they reflect the glorious landscapes through which the Cambrian railways ran, these have been included as part of the 'grand tour' of the Cambrian system. The technique required much painstaking effort from Andrew, and to give an example, the monochrome photograph of a 'Manor' in the Cambrian countryside is shown opposite together with Andrew's rendering of the scene in colour.

The book concentrates on these two photographic collections, with a short overview of the history of the routes that were part of the Cambrian Railway at its absorption by the Great Western Railway in 1922. For those seeking the full story, we commend the aforesaid volumes of R.W. Miller and Rex Christiansen published by David & Charles in 1967, and the comprehensive descriptions of the Cambrian by C.C. Green and R.W. Kidmer. C.P. Gasquoine, in a book published in 1922, and still found in many railway library collections, also covers the Cambrian Railways' turbulent history in a style that is often graphic, amusing, ironic and at times, a little over the top! For those seeking photographic records of the Cambrian routes, books by C.C. Green (Ian Allan 1977 & 1981), Rex Kennedy (Ian Allan 1990) and Derek Lowe (Book Law Publications 2013) fulfil that aim admirably. Vic Mitchell and Keith Smith produced a book of photos of the branch lines around Wrexham (Middleton Press 2009), and Mike Lloyd covered the Tanat Valley Light Railway (Wild Swan 1990).

The same photograph enhanced by Andrew Dyke's colourisation process. (Andrew Dyke colourisation)

The authors would also like to thank the following for their information and support that have made this book possible:-

Dave Owen	
Brian Rowe	
John Morris	
John Dyke	
Colin Vaughan	
Rob Williams	Chairman, Cambrian Heritage Railways
Sheila Dee	Community Rail Officer, Chester and Shrewsbury Rail Partnership
Claire Williams	Partnership Development Officer, Cambrian Railway Partnership
Robert Robotham	NetworkRail
William Troughton	National Library of Wales
Dave Postle	Kidderminster Railway Museum
Bruce Oliver	
Laurence Waters	
Phil Williams (son of T.E. Williams)	

And, of course, Paul's wife Clare, who has spent many hours in Wales researching the book and proofreading it.

The authors have endeavoured to trace the copyright owners of all the photographs included, but if we have been mistaken or omitted anyone, please contact the publisher.

PREFACE

I have been a fan of the Cambrian Railways for some forty years. It started by buying a print that just looked idyllic to me and deciding that, wherever it was, I was going to find that location and take a current photograph of whatever was left. The scene was of 7801 *Anthony Manor* departing Barmouth Junction (Morfa Mawddach) with a down passenger train heading for Barmouth. The simple, timeless beauty of the area and that engine just appealed to me. A short time after, *Foxcote Manor* was rescued from Barry scrapyard and taken to the yard in Oswestry Station. This was the headquarters of the fledgling Cambrian Railways Society which I immediately joined. Further visits followed and I gradually discovered the passion and respect in which the legendary Cambrian Railways is held. Many more trips were spent in North Wales discovering the Cambrian Coast and the routes of the old Cambrian lines.

I felt that I wanted to share my enthusiasm for the Cambrian Railways by writing about them but was very conscious of doing it justice when so many excellent books had already been

David Maidment, Founder Ambassador of Railway Children and a guest of the Llangollen Railway management, is on the footplate of former Oswestry 4-6-0, 7822 *Foxcote Manor,* with Driver Graham Hoyland, Secretary of the 'Foxcote Manor Society', on the occasion of the heritage railway's autumn gala, 3 September 2016. (Gordon Heddon)

written. Recently, I had the good fortune to meet David Maidment, a remarkable man who, as well as creating the Railway Children charity, is also a prolific author of many fine books and was a greatly respected senior manager with British Railways. Over the course of several meetings and coffees I asked if he would consider writing this book with me and he has been kind enough to agree. I was keen to bring a 'personal touch' to the story, based on the characters I was lucky enough to meet during my many visits. David loves to research the history, infrastructure and locomotives and so the book content came together in a rather natural way.

There was further reason I felt that another Cambrian book might be of interest. I had purchased the first two volumes of the C.C. Green works on the Cambrian Railways and was eagerly awaiting the planned further two volumes. Sadly 'Rick' Green died with the third volume all but complete. I have been told that Rick had agreed to leave his work to the Cambrian Railways Society, but for various reasons this did not happen. Unfortunately, his last book was never published, and his photographs sold at auctions. This book attempts to fill in some of those gaps around Oswestry, as well as highlighting the many good things currently happening along the line.

**Paul Carpenter
September 2018**

7822 *Foxcote Manor* at Llangollen Railway Gala, 3 September 2016. (David Maidment)

INTRODUCTION

Driving through the modern-day market town of Oswestry, you cannot fail to notice the large and stately-looking building that is Oswestry Station. Once surrounded by other buildings and even an adjoining station, it now stands alone, isolated but defiant. Its architecture and elegance suggest a history of a bygone age that was brimming with ambition, vision and wealth. Opened in 1860, this Victorian building wasn't merely the station building of the town but also the Headquarters of the Cambrian Railways.

The geography of this region is generally uncompromising, and it quickly becomes very challenging as you head west towards the Cambrian Coast. The directors who occupied the boardroom in that headquarters clearly recognised the business opportunities in constructing a railway across the Cambrian Mountains to the coast. They anticipated that there would be a demand for holiday traffic

Oswestry station devoid of trains after closure of the Cambrian Railways system at this location and the impressive station building and offices which once housed the headquarters of the Cambrian Railway Company, 1970. (Colour-Rail)

from the northern cities of Manchester, Liverpool and Birmingham and even cities as far away as London. Together with extensive farming in the area, as well as mineral deposits, freight receipts would be lucrative for an efficient railway.

This book looks at the characters who turned this vision into reality. It looks at the infrastructure they created, the engineering challenges they overcame, the locomotives and rolling stock they provided and how this changed the employment activities of the town. The life of the railway is traced through three changes in ownership and reflects on how these impacted upon the local community and daily life in the region. Uniquely, this book also juxtaposes the vision of those early day entrepreneurs with present day activities that have led to a fourth change of ownership and a revival in fortunes. The parallels with the struggles to build 'then and now' are evident, each with the wealth and prosperity of the town as its prize.

With the loss of the passenger services and the eventual closure of the whole line around Oswestry, a small group of enthusiasts have struggled for many years to recreate and reopen that part of the old Cambrian Railways system. This book reflects on the various ways this was attempted and how this has evolved and developed into the present and most successful period. Finally, the book captures the human side of this story by presenting conversations with some of the characters who have battled to recreate a Cambrian Heritage Railway and how they visualise the future for this noble line with its refurbished headquarters building.

The construction of the Cambrian Railways is a story of vision and determination overcoming natural obstructions and economic instability. It tells of how the railway historically became the major source of employment, business and social travel and how the region suffered when this was removed. The Welsh government has recognised the importance of an efficient transport system for the country and has ensured that the new rail franchise operator works closely with the communities to meet their needs.

Let's hope that we will soon witness the second coming of Cambrian Railways in this beautiful part of the world.

THE CAMBRIAN RAILWAYS – A BRIEF HISTORY TO 1922

It began as a grandiose idea of a railway through the centre of Wales to connect England with Ireland and spluttered into life as a twelve-mile single line between two small market towns with populations of less than 5,000 each twenty-five years later. In the meantime, the Great Western Railway had pushed through from Newport and Cardiff to Swansea and George Stephenson and the Chester & Crewe Railway (later part of the London & North Western) had opened up the North Wales Coast route and established the main contact with Ireland through the port at Holyhead. Ideas of a port in Cardigan Bay at Aberdovey or on the south of the Lleyn Peninsular at Port Dinlleyn had perished.

The British government had set up the Irish Railways Commission in 1836 to explore the best way of connecting England to Ireland by rail and sea, and routes from Shrewsbury through central Wales to the Lleyn Peninsular. A Brunel broad gauge option from Worcester via Montgomery and Newtown through the mountains at Talerddig to Dinas Mawddwy got mired in arguments about the terrain and finances by different vested interests, while the northern and southern main lines through Wales progressed. One of the vested interests that stymied progress was the band of canal owners who came together in 1845 to see off the railway threat. As well as the East-West routes in the north and south, the Shrewsbury, Oswestry and Chester Railway was constructing what was to become the northern end of the Great Western Railway's route from Birmingham to Shrewsbury and Chester. However, in 1846 a three-mile connection was built from Gobowen on the main line to the town of Oswestry, which would later become the headquarters of the Cambrian Railways – but not for many years yet.

There was a flurry of proposals developed and presented to parliament around 1852-3 – a Montgomeryshire Railway plan to build a railway from Shrewsbury to Aberystwyth and a proposed extension of the Shrewsbury & Chester Railway's Oswestry branch. However, these were rejected and the only proposal that cleared the parliamentary hurdle at this time was the modest plan to connect Llanidloes (at that time a prosperous town of 4,500 people with a thriving 'flannel' trade) with the market town of Newtown (population 4,000). Even that scheme was initially rejected by the House of Lords because of some rather fundamental flaws in the engineering plan which showed the line at one point to be eighteen feet below the waters of the River Severn. After correction, the twelve-mile line, intended long term as part of a route from Manchester to Milford Haven, was approved but only after much lobbying on its behalf by George Hammond Whalley, a descendant of Oliver Cromwell and John Hampden, who was High Sheriff of Caernarvonshire and MP for Peterborough, one of the larger than life characters who were embroiled in the early years of creating the railways that later formed the 'Cambrian'.

The scheme received parliamentary sanction in August 1853 and Mr Whalley became chairman of the Llanidloes & Newtown Railway Board. The single line was to have intermediate stations (from the Newtown end) at Scafell, Caersws, Llandinam, and Dolwen and the line rose from Newtown to Llanidloes steadily at gradients of around 1 in 220 interspersed with slightly easier sections. The prospectus envisaged an annual revenue of £8,250 of which some 30 per cent was from passengers, the freight traffic made up of lead, copper, coal, timber, agricultural produce, wool, cattle and sheep and general merchandise. Working expenses were calculated as only 50 per cent of the revenue, giving a 7 per cent return on the £60,000 capital sum to be invested.

C.P. Gasquoine, editor of the *Border Counties Advertizer*, wrote a biography of the Cambrian Railways in 1922 and his description of the events and the opening of the railway is couched in the flowery language of the time with a hint of irony that puts much colour into a confusing story of politics, lawsuits, cut-throat competition, rivalries, petty jealousies and bankruptcies, offset by the joyous welcoming of the new railway and its 'new-fangled monsters'. The first sod was to be cut at Llanidloes on 3 October 1855 and the lady who was to undertake the ceremony flew into high dudgeon when she saw what she thought was a premature announcement of her role before she had secured the presence of her influential friends and had reassured herself about the financial stability of the project. The local political storm was copied by the weather, so Mr Whalley himself had to cut the first sod in the deluge of a Welsh rainstorm.

The contract to construct the line was awarded to a local engineer, David Davies, of Llandinam, who had little schooling, but according to Gasquoine was educated from the age of eleven at the 'University of Observation' from which he graduated with high honours. The Board's engineer, after the death of the first appointee, was Benjamin Piercy, who oversaw the construction,

and Davies was partnered by another significant character in the development of the 'Cambrian', Thomas Savin. The line was opened for mineral traffic in April 1859 and the lady who had refused to cut the first sod, Mrs Owen of Glansevern, was persuaded to declare the line fully open to traffic on 31 August 1859. The celebrations included bell-ringing, cannon-firing and a march of 5,000 people extending a quarter of a mile to the station to greet the first train. During the rather long wait, the local band struck up 'See the Conquering Hero comes' and at last the VIPs took their seats in the train which set off for Newtown where it arrived shortly after midday, whereupon the party enjoyed a sumptuous feast – a routine established at all subsequent railway openings – and a succession of toasts and mutual congratulations extending well into the afternoon.

The statue of David Davies, educated at the 'University of Observation', standing beside the site of the first railway he constructed at the former Llandinam station, between Newtown and Llanidloes, June 2018. (David Maidment)

'Broneirion', the home of David Davies, construction engineer of the line from Newtown to Llanidloes, now headquarters of the Girl Guide movement of Wales. In June 2018, author David Maidment took a group of young people for a residential 'adventure weekend' to 'Broneirion'. (David Maidment)

The rather grandiose station of Llanidloes, the former headquarters of the 1861 Llanidloes & Newtown Railway, also the commencement of the Mid-Wales Railway southwards to Talyllyn Junction and Brecon. Subsequently, it was just a country station on the Llanidloes – Talyllyn Junction and Brecon line, served here by a two-coach local service from Newtown hauled by one of the ubiquitous Ivatt 2MT Swindon-built moguls that replaced the Dean Goods and Cambrian 0-6-0s in this area in the mid-1950s. (Andrew Dyke collection)

Llanidloes & Newtown Railway No.3, an 0-4-2T built for the line in 1859, originally named *Milford*, seen here after a cab had been fitted, c1891. It was one of four 0-4-2Ts built by Sharp, Stewart & Co., the other three being destined for the Vale of Clwyd Railway. It was one of the two locomotives that pulled the first passenger train at the official opening of the L&N on 31 August 1859. The engine was withdrawn in 1895. (MLS/R.W.Miller collection)

The return train set off belatedly after 3pm with forty-eight trucks and carriages, with an estimated 3,000 people on board, hauled by two of the company's four locomotives, 0-4-2Ts *Llewellyn* and *Milford*. It arrived at Llanidloes at 4pm and in the field adjoining the station, Mrs Owen at last declared the line to be open. Optimism was high as she declared that the railway would bring derelict areas into cultivation, that Llanidloes would be the very central town of the Principality, the capital of a new prosperity. There was then another feast with 300 sitting down to a somewhat belated lunch, followed by toasts to the Chairman, the Board Secretary, the Engineer, the Contractors, the Bankers and even to other railways mooted and being constructed elsewhere in the area. Finally, after the last toast to the Press, the somewhat inebriated party dispersed. There was even a six-verse song composed and sung for the occasion. The bard who composed it was awarded a shilling for his poetic effort. Everyone else in the crowd had a monster picnic in the field, with all the schoolchildren in a large

tent. The infant Cambrian Railway had been born.

The Llanidloes & Newtown Railway remained in isolation for just two years. However, during that time and even before then, rivalries between the Great Western and L&NWR in supporting and opposing various schemes to connect Oswestry or Shrewsbury with Newtown via Welshpool had delayed progress. When, finally, the Oswestry & Newtown Railway got its Parliamentary Bill to proceed, only eleven miles of track had been completed when the contractor was bankrupted. However, Davies and Savin, the contractors for the L&N, were now free of that commitment and undertook its completion with vigour. In the meantime, a Shrewsbury & Welshpool Railway Bill was passed in the House of Commons and the two schemes were progressed without co-operation – on the contrary, the period is noted for lawsuits, resignations, and general politicking with money being made and more often lost. To save money, it was decided after an inquiry led by a clergyman that the line from Welshpool to

Newtown should just be a single line, and that was followed with just small sections of double line between Oswestry and Llanymynech on the O&N and Buttington and Welshpool, where eventually the lines from Oswestry and Shrewsbury shared facilities.

To quote Gasquoine again, it was a long and tortuous story and one of perplexity to a local historian, 'when he turns over the files of the various newspapers, to see in one number the praises of certain gentlemen sung by admiring editors and enthusiastic correspondents, and in the next frantic outbursts from distracted shareholders against the devoted heads of the same gentlemen…' Davies and Savin had taken control of construction in October 1859 and by May 1860 one section of the line was opened from Oswestry. By the end of the month the track had nearly reached Welshpool and one evening, locomotive *Montgomery*, an 0-4-2, collected a string of trucks and people from the locality occupied every space available.

It proceeded to Cefn Junction where the line from Shrewsbury was being constructed and more trucks were added – plus a lot more passengers – and the whole cavalcade proceeded to the end of the line a mile or so short of Welshpool where speeches were made before everyone piled back in as the locomotive superintendent wanted to get back over the rough road before darkness fell. The train then went off 'at a smart pace' over unballasted track! The line from Oswestry to Welshpool was formally opened on 14 August 1860, with the usual celebrations of brass bands, marches, speeches, bell-ringing, eating, drinking and dancing.

Savin's first 0-4-2 No.4 *Wynnstay*, built by Sharp, Stewart in October 1859 for the Llanidloes & Newtown Railway and whose sister engine, No.5 *Montgomery*, hauled the first train of the Oswestry & Newtown Railway. Coupled wheels were 5ft diameter, cylinders 15½ x 22in, boiler pressure 120lbs psi, tractive effort, 9,023 lbs. The four-wheel tender held 1,200 gallons of water and 3 tons of coal. The engine weighed 24 tons 8 cwt. Initially just wooden brake blocks on the tender, this engine was later equipped with both steam and vacuum brake gear. (MLS/R.W.Miller collection)

The four-mile section from Newtown to Abermule was the first part of the O&N's route west of Welshpool to be completed but the intervening section was subject to the usual disputes and delays with local landowner objections to be overcome. Finally, on 27 May 1861, a train of engineers and invited guests ran between Welshpool and Newtown and a low-key opening (for the time) took place in typical pouring rain. Llanidloes was now connected to the outside world. Six trains a day ran every weekday from Oswestry to Llanidloes, one of which ran non-stop from Oswestry to Welshpool, and four returned daily. Two trains ran in each direction on Sundays, a most unusual development in the staunch chapel-going communities. The Shrewsbury and Welshpool Railway was completed shortly afterwards in January 1862 and then attention turned to further west.

A Newtown & Machynlleth Railway Bill was passed in July 1857 and construction of a 22-mile line was authorised at a cost of an estimated £150,000, the work to be completed within five years. Work began within a year of the formation of the company and the first sod was cut in Machynlleth accompanied by the usual celebrations – Gasquoine quotes 'a generous imbibing of a bountiful supply of prime port, sherry, etc., and a procession of miners and quarrymen who dined…at the White Lion Inn, the most noted house in the county for the excellence of its ale'. The construction of this line involved the cutting through of the mountains in the region of Talerddig, rising 273 feet from Caersws to 693 feet above sea level and then dropping 645 feet to the Dovey Valley. Two engines capable of hauling 140 tons up 1 in 52 gradients at 15mph were ordered from Sharp, Stewart & Co and in January 1863 the line opened with the two engines *Talerddig* and *Countess Vane* (named after the wife of the company's chairman) hauling a train containing 1,500 passengers from Machynlleth to Newtown and back. The return journey took two hours with celebrations in full swing at every intermediate station, finishing with speeches, luncheon, toasts and processing 'ad lib'…

One of the first batch of small 0-6-0s built by Sharp, Stewart to Thomas Savin's order for the Llanidloes & Newtown Railway, *Cambria*, later numbered Cambrian Railways 27, built in February 1863, at Machynlleth, c1875. No photos can be found of either 0-6-0 No.34 *Talerddig* or No.35 *Countess Vane*, built in December 1861, but they would have been similar in outline to No.27. (MLS/R.W. Miller collection)

Sharp, Stewart 2-4-0 No.30 *Albion* of 1863, as built. This was one of fourteen 2-4-0 tender engines built between 1863 and 1865 for the developing Cambrian railways. (MLS/R.W. Miller collection)

Sharp, Stewart 2-4-0 No.53 *Gladstone*, built in October 1865, at Oswestry c1880. (MLS/R.W. Miller collection)

The next step was to move on from Machynlleth to the 'Brighton of Wales' – Aberystwyth. A Bill to connect the two by the Aberystwyth & Welsh Coast Railway was passed by parliament in a remarkable two months, and despite opposition in other quarters who had designs on reaching the Welsh coast themselves or with their other allies. Thomas Savin and his brother commenced the twelve-mile section from Machynlleth over the marshes through Ynyslas to Borth.

Sharp, Stewart 0-4-2 No.7 *Llanerchydol* built in December 1860 for the L&N Railway, at Towyn on a train for Barmouth, with station and train crew posing for the occasion. It is fitted with a roofless cab and remained hand-braked only. Its name was removed in June 1891. (MLS/R.W. Miller collection)

The line was ready by July 1863 and the contractor at once tried to capitalise on the nearness of the sea by building a row of boarding houses which unfortunately soon sank into the swamp. Undeterred, Thomas Savin then tried his luck at Borth, previously a fishing village, and a day trip excursion train from Machynlleth to Borth took 100 passengers on an early morning departure. So great was the demand that a second train ran a few hours later, with 530 on board. The journey apparently took about twenty-five minutes. Through tickets from Shrewsbury and Oswestry were subsequently advertised for half-a-crown and scenes at Borth that August, according to Gasquoine, merited a Hogarth to depict. Moving on to Aberystwyth itself was a bit harder but was eventually accomplished by June 1864. In the meantime, opening up the coastal route from Aberdovey to Barmouth and Portmadoc was on the agenda and the stretch from Aberdovey to Llwyngwril was opened in October 1863.

The next section over the Friog cliffs where the flanks of the Cader Idris mountain come down to the sea caused more difficulty and delay, but Barmouth Junction, south of the Mawddach estuary, was reached in July 1865. This left the awkward swamp from the Ynyslas area around Glandovey across the Dovey estuary to the ferries for the moment and it was not until 1867 that that gap was filled. The wider Mawddach estuary was not bridged until 1867 either.

While efforts to open the coast were progressing, another battle was raging at the eastern border of Wales. A meeting was held in Ellesmere in October 1860 proposing a link to the

Crewe-Whitchurch line, thus giving access from the populous Lancashire towns to the Welsh coast. Then opposition from the GWR stirred and other promoters started envisaging a whole series of lines radiating from Ellesmere. Iron and coal owners in the area entered the fray and the proposed schemes around Ellesmere caused nothing but confusion. The L&NWR put its backing behind the Whitchurch-Oswestry scheme as it gave its company access to central Wales and would obstruct the GWR. The Whitchurch-Ellesmere section got the go-ahead in 1861, but the stretch on to Oswestry was delayed to 1862 to try to get accommodation with the Great Western's interests at Ruabon and Shrewsbury. The Whitchurch-Ellesmere section, including three difficult miles across Whixall Moss, was completed by April 1863 and work started on the Oswestry line. When the Machynlleth-Aberystwyth route opened in 1864, the Ellesmere-Oswestry section was the only gap in the line from Crewe and the north to the Welsh coast. When the opposition of the GWR was overcome and the final

approval was given, the church bells in Oswestry apparently rang out for two days. The extension on to Oswestry was completed over a year later in July 1864.

Four companies owned the route from Whitchurch to Aberystwyth – the Oswestry, Ellesmere & Whitchurch; the Oswestry & Newtown; the Newtown & Machynlleth; and the original Llanidloes & Newtown. Common Sense saw the need for close co-operation through the operation of the Oswestry & Newtown Joint Committee and this led directly to a Bill before parliament in March 1864 to enable these four railways to amalgamate as the 'Cambrian Railways'. The Bill was passed in July 1864 despite strong opposition – as usual – from the Great Western (although as we shall see, they lost the battle but eventually won the war). The new Cambrian Railways directors received a report by Earl Vane admitting that the aggressive policies of the 'Great Companies' had not been in the interests of other smaller companies or the public and that concentration on developing the traffic was now in the interests of all,

0-4-2, Mid-Wales Railway No.2, built by Kitson in November 1864, which became Cambrian Railways No.2 also when that railway operated the MWR in 1888 and was withdrawn in 1905. It was reboilered at Builth in 1887, remained on the Mid-Wales section and is seen here at Brecon, c1888. (MLS/R.W. Miller collection)

and commended co-operation with the Mid-Wales Railway that was opening up from Llanidloes southwards to Talyllyn and Brecon and the Aberystwyth & Welsh Coast Railway.

Earl Vane was elected Chairman of the Board in August. The L&NWR also found it in its interest to support the new railway and signed a running powers agreement through to Welshpool. The Aberystwyth & Welsh Coast Railway had missed out on the amalgamation for a technical reason but was shortly afterwards absorbed into the Cambrian Railways. The map of the Cambrian Railways in 1864 is illustrated opposite.

We now come to the development of the coastal section and the estuary gaps. Initially, it was intended to build a long bridge across the Dovey estuary to Aberdovey where ambitious minds envisaged a steamer service to Ireland. There were problems in finding a firm foundation on shifting sands and ebbing tides and this first attempt was abandoned. The proposed route was altered to cross the Dovey at a much narrower point near Glandovey and the new line diverted from the Aberystwyth line there at a remote location that was later Dovey Junction station – a station with no exit and whose only purpose was the exchange of passengers between the coastal lines to Aberystwyth and Barmouth. Dovey Junction was also peculiar in that it existed in three Welsh counties – the station itself was in Montgomeryshire, the station master's house nearby just over the river bridge was in Merioneth and an up distant signal on the Aberystwyth line worked from Dovey Junction signal box was in Cardiganshire.

The line from Aberdovey to Llwyngwril had been completed in 1863, despite having to counter flooding from high tides and storms where the track was little protected from the sea. The building of the line over the Friog cliffs had eventually been accomplished in 1865. The diversion to link Machynlleth with Aberdovey was finally achieved in August 1867.

However, there was no easy diversion available to cross the Mawddach estuary. Initially, trains turned inland south of the Mawddach river up to Penmaenpool half way to Dolgelley, where the train was met by ferries to cross the river. There was also a ferry at Barmouth Junction – the location is now known as Fairbourne. There was in the end no alternative but to bridge the estuary at its widest point. The river here was 800 yards wide and a bridge was constructed carried on 113 spans on 500 timber piles. The navigable part of the river on the Barmouth shore was crossed by an iron-work construction of seven fixed and one opening span of a drawbridge type that lifted at one end. This part of the bridge was renewed in 1899 with a modern steel structure of four spans. The bridge was completed and tested in July 1866, but it was not used by steam trains until October 1867.

The line to Portmadoc and Pwllheli was finally completed and opened in October 1867, though not without alarms as the main contractor, Thomas Savin, was bankrupted in February 1866 and the Cambrian was left to complete the work from its own resources, with a substantial (but reluctant) bank loan. The proposed extension to the long-desired port for Ireland, Porth Dinlleyn, was never reached. The extension from Penmaenpool to Dolgelley was opened in June 1868, linking up with the GWR line from Ruabon, Llangollen and Bala at Dolgelley in August 1869. In the intervening years branches had sprung up off the Cambrian main line to Porthywaen, Kerry and Llanfyllin, and a small independently owned railway had opened – the Mawddwy Railway – in 1867 for passengers and goods (mainly slate).

Despite the completion of the main route, following Savin's bankruptcies and legal disputes over moneys owing between the various parties, the Cambrian Railway was in no great shape financially. It was struggling. The Cambrian's revenue share from the coastal section was not covering its costs, expensive lawsuits

CARNARVON

BIRKENHEAD CHESTER CREWE

DENBIGH

LLANDUDNO

WREXHAM (Central)
Marchwiel
WHITCHURCH

LNW

Bangor-on-Dee
Fenns Bank

Overton-on-Dee
Bettisfield
Welshampton

ELLESMERE
Frankton

PWLLHELI
Abererch
Afonwen
Criccieth
Wern
PORTMADOC
Mintffordd

BLAENAU FESTINIOG

RUABON

CHIRK

Whittington

OSWESTRY

Penrhyndeudraeth
Talsarnau
Harlech

CORWEN

Llynclys
Pant

SHREWSBURY

Llanbedr

BALA

Llangynog
Penybontfawr
Pedair-Ffordd
Llanrhaiadr-Mochnant
Pentrefelin
Porthywaen
Nantmawr
Blodwell Jn

LLANYMYNECH

WELLING

Dyffryn

TVLR

Llangedwyn
Llanstin Rd
Glanyrafon
Llany-blodwell R

Four Crosses
Arddleen

S&MLR

GW/LNW

BARMOUTH
Barmouth Jn
Penmaen Pool

Dinas Mawddwy

Llanfyllin
Bryngwyn
Llanfechan
Llansantffraid
Pool Quay
Seven Stars

Buttington

BUILD.

CARDIGAN BAY

Fairbourne
Llwyngwril

Arthog
DOLGELLEY
Corris

Mallwyd
Aberangell
Cemmaes

Llanfair Caereinion
Cyfronydd
Cas-Caereinion
Sylfaen Golfa
Raven Sq.

WELSHPOOL

GW

CR

Cemmes Road

Tonfanau

TR

Glandyfi
MACHYNLLETH
Dovey Jn

Llanbryn-mair
Talerddig
Carno

Forden

MONTGOMERY

TOWYN
ABERDOVEY

Ynys Las
Borth
Llandre

Pontdolgogh
Trewythan
Red House

Caersws
Moat Lane Jn
Scafell (gds)

Abermule

NEWTOWN
Kerry

Craven Arms

Bow Street

Van
Garth Rd
Cerist

Trefeg-lwys

Llandinam

Bishop's Castle

ABERYSTWYTH
Llanbadarn
Glanrafon
Capel Bangor
Nantyronen
Aberffrwyd
Rheidol Falls
Rhiwfron

Dolwen
LLANIDLOES

HEREFORD

Devil's Bridge

Tylwch

Pantydwr
St Harmons

GW

TREGARON

RHAYADER

LNW

Doldowlod

CARMARTHEN

Newbridge-on-Wye

HEREFORD

Builth Road
BUILTH WELLS

MR

Aberedw

Erwood HAY

GW

PONTRILAS

LLANDOVERY

CAMBRIAN RAILWAYS 1864

Boughrood & Llyswen

Three Cocks Jn

CAMBRIAN RAILWAYS

OTHER LINES

TALGARTH
Trefeinon

N&B BRECON B&M

R = RHYDMEREDYDD

Scale 0   10   20 Miles
Approx

MERTHYR

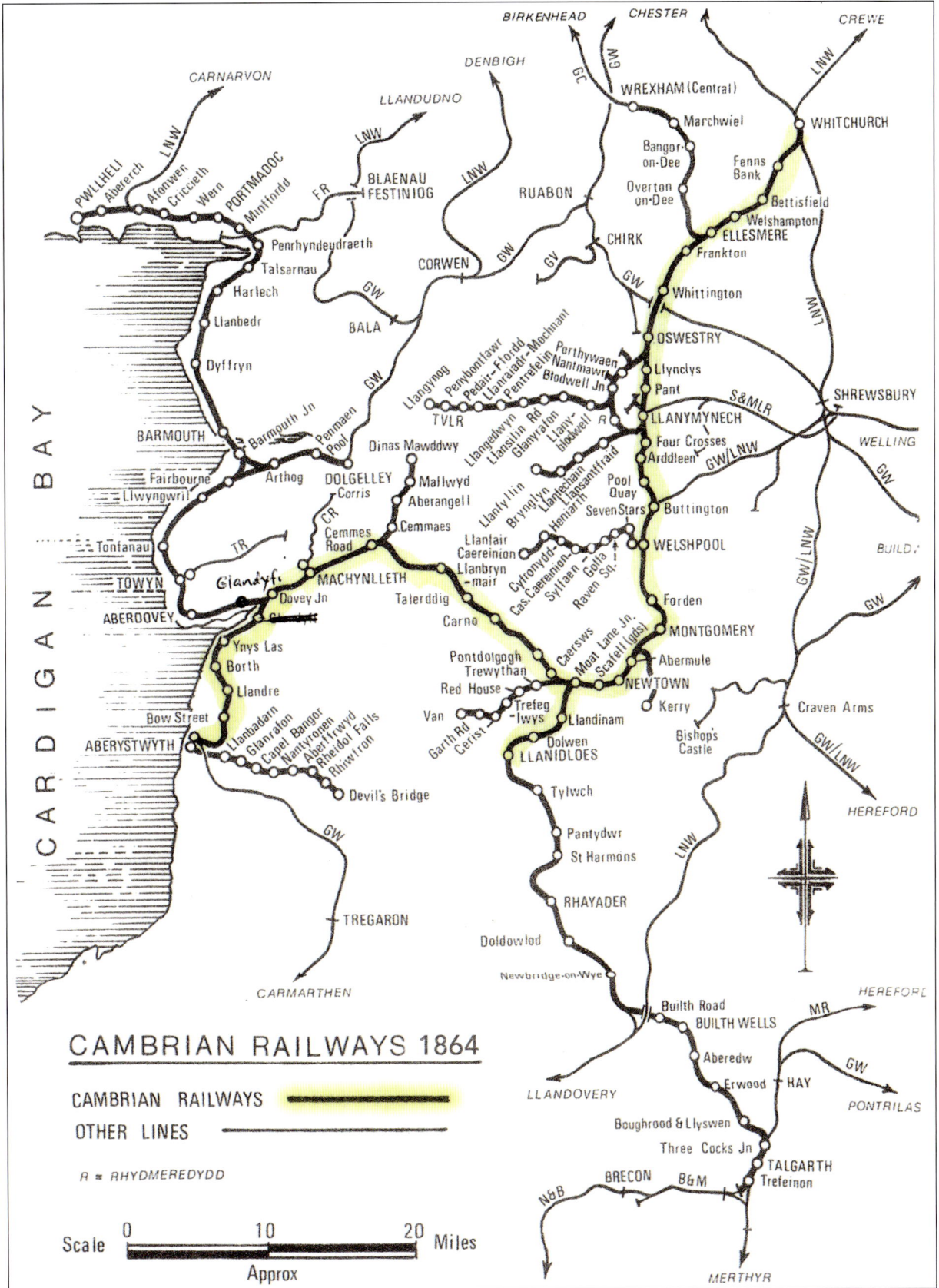

The Newtown & Llanidloes, the Oswestry & Newtown, the Newtown & Aberystwyth and
Whitchurch –Oswestry independent lines that formed the Cambrian Railways in 1864.

Sharp, Stewart 0-4-0ST No.36 *Plasfynnon* built in 1863, at Kerry with a mixed train, c1900. (MLS/R.W. Miller collection)

Manning Wardle 0-6-0ST *Mawddwy* built for the construction of the Potteries, Shrewsbury and North Wales Railway, originally named *Alyn,* and sold in 1867 to the Cemmes Road-Dinas Mawddwy light railway, reboilered in 1893 and seen here in 1895. It was numbered No.30 and taken into Cambrian stock in 1913 and renumbered by the GWR as 824, only being withdrawn in September 1940. After working the Tanat Valley branch for a time, it spent its last few years at Moat Lane on the Van branch, though its GWR mileage was only just under 58,000 miles. (MLS/R.W. Miller collection)

with claims and counter-claims abounded and the shareholders were getting restive as they were now looking to the operating railway to bring the rewards from their investment. The Company was bankrupted in 1868 and recovered very slowly through the 1870s.

The routes that became the Cambrian Railways were now more or less settled. In later years it worked the Llanymynech-Nantmawr branch and the Llanidloes-Talyllyn line built by the Mid-Wales Railway. The route mileage was 180, plus the 51 miles that it operated for the two other railways mentioned above. It continued to struggle financially. Not much was spent on track or loco maintenance to 1880, the slate industry became depressed and the flannel trade in Newtown declined from 1883. It was bankrupted again in 1884, discharged in 1885. Some modernisation with decent track took place between 1883 and 1885.

However, things began to improve in the 1880s. Train services were improving and summer traffic to the coast was increasing. The populations of the West Midlands industrial cities and towns discovered the seaside holiday and Aberystwyth and Barmouth attracted seasonal traffic. The locomotive stock was increased to cope, with thirty-three new locomotives being built in the 1880s and 1890s and thirty-one older engines being rebuilt. The company was able to invest in bogie coaches, vacuum brakes and better signalling.

The prototype Small Bogie 4-4-0, No.16 *Beaconsfield*, designed and constructed by Sharp, Stewart &Co. in 1878, with 5ft 6½in coupled wheels, two 17x 24in inside cylinders, 140lb psi boiler pressure, giving 12,412lbs tractive effort and weighing 33 tons 3 cwt without tender. No.16 was reboiled in 1913. Engines of this class were employed on the Llanidloes-Brecon route regularly from 1898. No.16's name was removed in December 1891 and it was renumbered 1115 by the GWR and withdrawn in January 1925. This photo was taken at Llanidloes prior to 1891. (MLS/R.W. Miller collection)

'Large Bogie' No.69, built February 1894 by Sharp, Stewart & Co., reboilered in May 1912, withdrawn as GW No.1102 in December 1925, June 1912. The coupled wheels were 6ft diameter, the cylinders 18 x 24in and boiler pressure of 150 lbs psi, giving tractive effort of 13,770 lbs. The engine weighed 40 tons 5 cwt and the 2,500-gallon tender carrying 4 tons of coal, 30 tons. They superseded the 2-4-0s and 'small bogie' 4-4-0s on main line duties and from 1903 on the coastal section and 1905 on the Mid-Wales Railway where they were the heaviest engines allowed. (MLS/R.W. Miller collection)

As yet there was no motor traffic to compete. Many of the older directors retired and were replaced by new blood and new ideas were accepted with the cross-fertilisation as senior appointments were made with experience of other railway companies. There were some hiccups – the hours and conditions for the Cambrian Railways' staff were becoming challenged and the 'Hood' incident – the appearance of a station master before a parliament committee to give evidence of excessive hours worked by staff – caused problems for the company and unrest amongst the staff, leading to the strengthening of the trade union movement and a challenge the directors were forced to face.

The railway's operations continued to react to opportunities and pressures. The paddle-steamer service that had been introduced between Aberdovey

and Waterford in 1889 with enthusiasm, opening up a new route to Ireland, was short-lived when the L&NWR slashed rates via Holyhead. There was a 'Welsh Railways Through Traffic Act' in 1889 which promoted co-operation between railways in the area – the Chester & Connah's Quay, the Wrexham, Mold & Connah's Quay, the Ellesmere-Wrexham line and further south, the Neath & Brecon. Although the GWR was dominant in the Wrexham area, the Cambrian worked the Ellesmere-Wrexham line, opened in November 1895, for 55 per cent of the gross receipts. This route failed to meet expectations, but it did at least furnish a modest profit.

More feeder services to the main lines were built in the 1890s, stimulated in particular by the 1896 Light Railways Act. The Van Railway which fed into the

Mid-Wales line on the slopes of Plynlimon, built back in 1870, was taken over after it had been declared bankrupt in 1893 – it was a source of ballast for the Cambrian Railways and reopened in 1896.

The Elan Valley Railway was started in 1892 and completed in 1896 to aid construction of the Birmingham City Water company dam and was operated by the Cambrian Railways until completion of the project – the dam was opened by Edward VII in 1904, the line was partly lifted in 1906 and totally closed in 1916. Nantmawr was reached off the Llanfyllin branch

Manning Wardle 0-6-0ST built as No.2 of the Van Railway and absorbed by the Cambrian Railway in 1896 and renumbered 25, seen here with local staff at Cemmes Road in 1910. It was sold to the government in 1917 and was offered for further sale in 1922. (MLS/R.W. Miller collection)

Hunslet Contractor's 0-6-0ST *Nantgwyllt* built for the Elan Valley branch, with Mid-Wales Railway brake van, July 1904. (MLS/R.W. Miller collection)

in 1896 and the Tanat Valley Railway opened in 1904. However, the populations served by these branches were sparse and therefore the lines were uneconomic, so other ideas were tried. The Cambrian Railways pioneered the use of motor bus services to provide feeders to its trains after a successful Bill in 1903 and two vehicles plied a service between Pwllheli and Nevin and Porth Dinlleyn in 1906 (and later a service to Beddgelert). The narrow-gauge railways the Welshpool & Llanfair and Vale of Rheidol were constructed.

Although the Cambrian Railway had been operating the Mid-Wales Railway from Llanidloes to Talyllyn and Brecon since 1888, the position was consolidated in 1904 when that railway was amalgamated fully with the Cambrian; the negotiations had been going on secretly for some time in an attempt to avoid unwelcome intervention by either the L&NWR or GWR. From 1900, more investment was made to improve the railway's infrastructure to meet the increased traffic demands. Heavier rail was used on the main line, bridges and culverts were further strengthened, the Barmouth bridge was reconstructed at the navigable side of the Mawddach estuary at a cost of £60,000.

Between 1889 and 1913 passenger miles had increased by 73 per cent, freight tonnage by 92 per cent and revenue by 35 per cent. However, towards the end of the first decade of the new century, working hours and wages of staff were improved after further industrial unrest and the growing power of the trade unions, both nationally and locally. Costs were increasing, and financial reforms were necessary in the running of the company, although such activity was overtaken by the onset of the First World War and government take-over of the nation's railway system. Many armed forces training camps were set up in Wales – Rhayader, Aberystwyth and Portmadoc were the most important – and military traffic was heavy, taking advantage of the doubling of the Moat Lane-Newtown section (undertaken in 1912 to cater for the growing summer traffic). It is estimated that the Cambrian moved 250,000 troops during the war as well as much heavy freight, including acting as a relief route for steam coal from South Wales to the navy's base at Scapa Flow – the 'Jellicoes'.

There was a national rail strike in 1917, followed by an unpopular 50 per cent increase in passenger fares, and the railway struggled in the latter years of the war with substantially reduced staffing. In 1914, the railway had employed 1,912 staff, but 451 of them had enlisted in the forces and 53 were subsequently killed in action. At the end of the war, industrial unrest increased, and the railway suffered a couple of years of intermittent strikes, culminating in the 1921 national miners' strike supported by railwaymen. Then in 1921, the Cambrian Railway's reputation was further marred by the tragic head-on collision at Abermule which destroyed two of its most modern locomotives and killed fifteen passengers, including one of the company's directors.

Despite these adverse events, the Cambrian Railways had made a modest profit of £122,000 in its last year of independent existence from the carriage of 2.1 million passengers and 700,000 tons of freight. The Railways Act of August 1921 brought about the 'Grouping' into the 'Big Four', but a year before the full amalgamation, the Welsh railways, including the Cambrian, were 'absorbed' by the Great Western Railway from January 1922, although the actual implementation date for the Cambrian was 25 March 1922. The GWR inherited a capital of £6.5 million, revenue income of £414,000, 3,853 shareholders, 295 miles of route track, 99 steam locomotives and 2,690 passenger and freight rolling stock vehicles. One Cambrian Railways Director, David Davies, was brought on to the GWR Board.

Despite all the intervening skirmishes, the Great Western had finally won the war, and it was now up to the new company to develop the Cambrian railways.

'Large bogie' No.82, built in May 1895, on the Cambrian at an unidentified location, c1920, shortly before it was destroyed in the head-on collision at Abermule in January 1921. (MLS/R.W. Miller collection/A.G. Ellis)

'Large Belpaire' No.95, built in July 1904, at Oswestry, 28 June 1909. No.95 was destroyed in the Abermule head-on collision in January 1921 and was scrapped at the location. (MLS/R.W. Miller collection)

The Cambrian Railways System in 1922.

CAMBRIAN RAILWAYS

| CAMBRIAN RAILWAYS | ———— |
| OTHER LINES | ———— |

R = RHYDMEREDYDD

Scale 0   10   20 Miles
Approx

The lines of the Cambrian Railways at January 1922 when absorbed by the Great Western Railway

GALLERY OF PHOTOS OF CAMBRIAN LOCOMOTIVES

R.W. (Bob) Miller was Chairman of the Manchester Locomotive Society (MLS), whose clubrooms are on Stockport station, and was a great enthusiast for local railways, particularly the Cheshire Lines Committee (CLC) railways and the Cambrian. Over the years, he amassed a huge collection of photographs, many from very early days, especially Great Western, including Broad Gauge, and on his death these were bequeathed to the MLS.

Some have been published, but the majority have not been, and the following pages share these images of the Cambrian locomotive fleet. All the photos in this chapter are from Bob Miller's collection, made available by the MLS Archivist, Paul Shackcloth, and no publication fee has been requested as all the royalties from this book are being donated to the Railway Children charity. Any photos from other sources, where known, have been credited after the caption.

Passenger locomotives

The first Sharp, Stewart 2-4-0 built in March 1863 to the order of Thomas Savin for the Oswestry & Newtown Joint Committee, No.28, named *Mazeppa*, c1875. Built at first with weatherboards rather than a cab and braked only by wooden blocks on the tender wheels, it and its eleven sisters had 5ft 6in coupled wheels, two inside 16x20in cylinders, 120 lb psi boiler pressure and with a tender holding 1,200 gallons weighed 41 tons 12 cwt. These engines were the mainstay of the Cambrian system before this type of work was taken over by the Cambrian 4-4-0s in the 1880s. It was reboilered in June 1893, and is seen here at Machynlleth, 29 June 1909. (MLS/R.W. Miller collection/H.L. Hopwood)

Sharp, Stewart 2-4-0, No.41, built in March 1864 for the Oswestry & Newtown Joint Committee, initially named *Cader Idris* but renamed *Countess Vane* after the Chairman's wife (name transferred from an 0-6-0 goods engine, thought inappropriate for the Chairman's wife!) seen here at Aberdovey, c1903. No.41 was reboilered in 1893 and name removed, allocated to 'surplus stock' in 1906, but then survived to be taken over by the GWR though never receiving its allocated new number, 1330, being condemned in July 1922.

Sharp, Stewart 2-4-0 No.42, formerly *Glandovey*, immediately after reboilering in June 1891, at Oswestry.

Sharp, Stewart 2-4-0 No.53 at Oswestry before reboilering, March 1889.

Sharp, Stewart 2-4-0 No.54 crosses Barmouth Bridge towards Barmouth Junction with a train for Machynlleth, c1900. (MLS/Dr T.F. Baddam)

Sharp, Stewart
2-4-0, No.55,
formerly named
Treflach, built in
1865, reboilered and
fitted with an Aston
chimney in 1894,
stored in October
1916, allotted
GW No.1333,
but withdrawn
in November
1922 before
carried, at Harlech,
c1911. (MLS)

Cambrian Railways No.34, formerly Metropolitan Railway No.13, at Machynlleth where it was based until rebuilding in 1915, when it was one of two former Met tanks rebuilt as a 4-4-0. It was one of five former Beyer, Peacock 4-4-0Ts, built in 1864, and purchased by the Cambrian in November 1905 at the bargain price of £500 after they were made redundant on the Metropolitan Railway by electrification. Their condensing gear was removed, and this locomotive was based at Machynlleth performing local passenger work to Aberystwyth and Barmouth.

No.34, as rebuilt in 1915 as a 4-4-0, one of the two Met tanks (No.36 was the second) purchased by the Cambrian Railways in 1905. It was allocated GWR No. 1113, but this was never carried as it was withdrawn just two months after amalgamation in May 1922. It is seen here at Aberystwyth, 24 July 1920.

'Small Bogie' No.21 built in July 1886 to the Sharp, Stewart 1878 design (see photo of the prototype No.16 *Beaconsfield* earlier, page 25), poses after reboilering at Oswestry in October 1910.

Cambrian 'Small Bogie' 4-4-0, No.50, renumbered 1110 in 1922 and withdrawn in January 1925. It is languishing here in the 'Swindon Dump' awaiting cutting up along with a 'Bulldog' 4-4-0. The absence of tender allows a full view of the footplate controls. (MLS/R.W. Miller collection/A.G. Ellis)

Large Bogie ('61' class) No.19, built at Oswestry in 1901 to the Sharp, Stewart design of 1893. The coupled wheels were 6ft diameter, the cylinders 18x24in and boiler pressure of 150 lbs psi, giving tractive effort of 13,770 lbs. The engine weighed 40 tons 5 cwt and the 2,500-gallon tender, carrying 4 tons of coal, 30 tons. They superseded the 2-4-0s and 'Small Bogie' 4-4-0s on main line duties and from 1903 on the coastal section and 1905 on the Mid-Wales Railway where they were the heaviest engines allowed. The Works had found two spare boilers in 1899 and the new Locomotive Superintendent, Herbert Jones, was authorised to construct two locomotives to this design, No.19 being the first. It is seen here in Aberdovey, c1903.

'Large Bogie' No.83, built by Sharp, Stewart in May 1895, reboilered in 1921, photographed shortly afterwards at Oswestry. This locomotive had an excellent reputation and was used for Cambrian Railways royals and was used on the *Cambrian Coast Express* when introduced by the GWR. As GW 1106, renumbered again as 1110 in 1926, it was the last survivor of its class, being withdrawn in April 1931, offered on the 'Sales List' and not scrapped until 1934.

'Large Bogie' No.84, built by Sharp, Stewart & Co. in 1895, seen from the other side, at Aberystwyth, c1920. (MLS)

'Large Bogie' No.32, one of four built by R. Stephenson & Co. in 1897-8, on the turntable at Oswestry, c1911. (MLS)

The last 'Large Bogie' 4-4-0, No.11, one of two built at Oswestry Works in July 1904, photographed at Barmouth, c1905.

CAMBRIAN RAILWAYS. 1893

A passenger 4-4-0 designed by Aston.

A colour postcard of 'Large Bogie' 4-4-0 No.82, designed by Aston in 1893.

'Large Belpaire' Passenger 4-4-0, No.94, in Works grey, built in July 1904, the first of five 4-4-0s ordered from R. Stephenson & Co. in 1903. This example was renumbered by the GWR as 1014 and was withdrawn in April 1928. The coupled wheels were 6ft diameter, the two inside cylinders 18½x26in, boiler pressure 170 lbs psi, and weighed 45 tons 5 cwt plus tender at 31 tons 13 cwt. This class was restricted to the Whitchurch/Oswestry-Machynlleth main line until 1915 when track strengthening allowed them to gain route availability over the coastal sections.

'Large Belpaire'
No.98 (later
GW 1043) at
Aberystwyth, c1920.

A superb model of 'Large Belpaire Passenger' No.98 in Cambrian livery, constructed at Oswestry Works in 1907 to 1½in to 1ft scale, 7¼in gauge.

'Large Belpaire' 4-4-0 GW No.1029, formerly Cambrian Railways No.96, built in November 1904, shortly after the Cambrian's absorption by the GWR, c1923. The engine has received the new number but is still in Cambrian Railways livery. The engine, with 1014, was based at Oswestry.

'61' class large bogie 1093 (Cambrian Railways No.64), built in 1893, just repainted after absorption by the GWR, withdrawn in April 1926, c1923.

Former GW 2-4-0 No.212, built at Wolverhampton in 1883. This was one of two that had been in store and were purchased by the Cambrian Railway in 1921 and given the numbers 1 and 10. No.1 was given the GW number 1329 and worked from Machynlleth on the coast section until withdrawn in 1927. (MLS/W. Potter)

'Large Belpaire' 4-4-0 No.1043 (Cambrian Railways No.98), modified at Swindon in 1926, being the only one of the class to be superheated, receive a new smokebox, and cylinders. Boiler pressure was raised to 180 lbs psi and the heating surface was increased. It was based at Aberystwyth with 1035 (ex-No.97) but when the other three locomotives of the class were withdrawn in 1928, it moved to Oswestry until it was withdrawn in 1933 and stored on the GWR's 'Sales List' as it was still in reasonable condition. However, no buyers were found, and it was cut up a few months later having run 178,166 miles in GWR ownership.

One of the class '3521' 4-4-0s rebuilt by Churchward in 1900 from Dean 0-4-4Ts built in 1888, No.3545, that was transferred to the Cambrian in 1921 as a replacement for the two Cambrian 4-4-0s destroyed in the Abermule accident. 3545 is seen here at Machynlleth, c1930. It was withdrawn in 1931 having run just under a million miles. (MLS)

The Cambrian engines' successors were the GW 1895 'Dukes' and the first to arrive on the Central Wales Division of the Great Western was 3271 *Eddystone*, berthed here at Machynlleth shed in the early 1920s. (GW Trust)

Great Western Steam Motor No.78 of the type that was used on the Barmouth-Dolgelley services and other Cambrian branches in the early 1920s, photographed at Oswestry. (Andrew Dyke Collection)

Freight tender locomotives

Llanidloes & Newtown Railway No.2 *Ruthin* was a small 0-4-0 tender ballast engine built in 1860 by Manning, Wardle & Co. for construction of the Denbigh, Ruthin and Corwen Railway. Wheels were 4ft in diameter, outside cylinders 14x18in and the wooden framed four-wheel tender held 750 gallons of water. It lost its name in 1866 and was used as a ballast engine in the Oswestry area until 1878. It was then idle until withdrawal in 1886 but was not scrapped until 1894.

'Small Goods' Sharp, Stewart 0-6-0 No.6 *Marquis* at Oswestry, March 1889, before rebuilding (in 1895) and losing its name. No.6 was built in July 1873.

No.6 with a passenger train at Llanymynech, 1904. (MLS/W.E. Fox-Davies)

'Small Goods' Sharp, Stewart 0-6-0, No.1, initially named *Victoria*, built in June 1872, rebuilt in 1891 and seen here immediately afterwards at Oswestry.

'Small Goods' No.39, built in June 1863 and named *Sir Watkin*, seen here at Aberdovey Quay branch, after reboilering in the 1890s, c1911.

The former 'Small Goods' No.14 in GW days as No.898 at Machynlleth, c1938. It survived until the month before nationalisation – a life of seventy-three active years. (MLS/Real Photographs)

1864 built 'Small Goods' No.900 at Portmadoc, c1935. (Andrew Dyke collection)

'Small Goods' 910, formerly Cambrian No.51, *Snowdon*, reboilered in 1894, with a freight at Oswestry, c1925. It has acquired a large Cambrian tender from a withdrawn 'Large Belpaire' 0-6-0 or 4-4-0.

The second Aston '73' class 0-6-0, No.74, built in May 1894, in Works grey livery, immediately after construction. It entered GW ownership as No.876 and was withdrawn in May 1946. (MLS/R.W. Miller collection/Bryan Jackson)

Aston 0-6-0 No.74 in early Cambrian Railways livery ex-works at Oswestry, c1894. (MLS/F. Moore)

Class '73' 0-6-0 No.80, built in September 1895, at Oswestry shortly after construction. It became GWR No.883 and was offered for sale in November 1926, being surplus to requirements.

'Large Belpaire Goods' No.99 at Machynlleth, 15 August 1913. During its first six months from March-October 1908, it was numbered '15' giving the class name, then was renumbered, and in GW times was 893, surviving nationalisation until withdrawn in February 1953.

Driver Tom Caffrey at the controls of 'Large Belpaire Goods' No.102, 4 July 1913.
(MLS/R.W. Miller collection/ H.W. Burman)

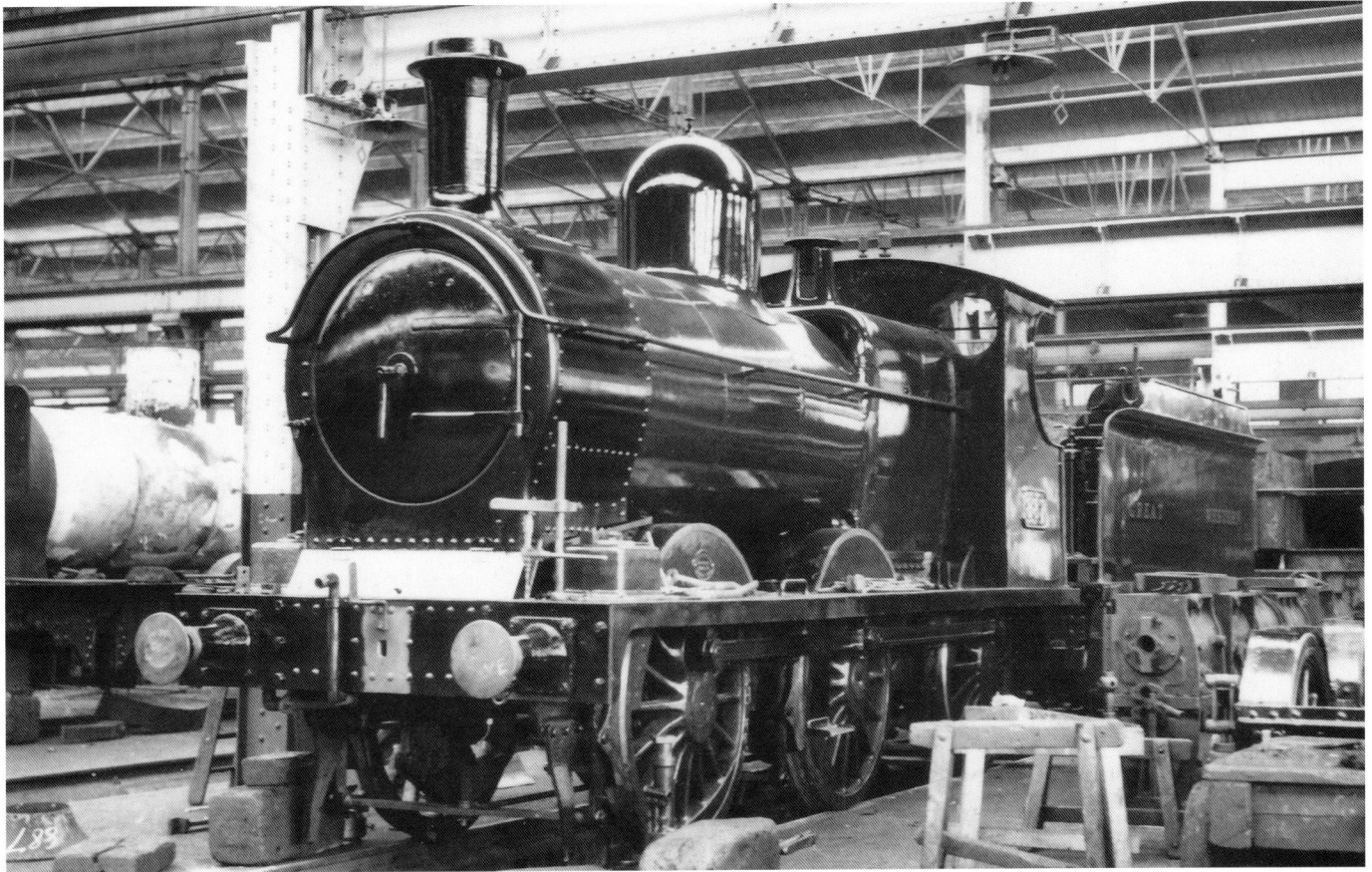

The prototype of the large Belpaire 0-6-0 goods, No.15, designed in 1903, was designated class '15', but was renumbered 89 in 1908 and 887 in 1922. It is shown here being reboilered in Swindon Works in April 1932.

GW No.855, formerly Cambrian Railways No.31, built by Beyer, Peacock in May 1919 to the Jones 1903 design, ex-works in GWR livery, October 1924. 855 was not withdrawn until October 1954. This class had 5ft 1½in wheels, 18x26in cylinders and boiler pressure of 160 lbs psi, giving a tractive effort of 18,630 lbs. Engine and tender weighed 73 tons 6 cwt.

GW 844, of the Jones '15' class 0-6-0 1903 design, built in October 1918 by Beyer, Peacock. 844 is photographed here at Oswestry shed alongside 'Dukedog' 3216 on 15 May 1938 and was withdrawn as BR (WR)844 in August 1954. (MLS)

Tank engines

Three small 2-4-0 side tanks were ordered by Thomas Savin and delivered in May 1866. The first was No.57 *Maglona* rebuilt in 1893. It is pictured here at Llanidloes in 1896 before removal of the name. It became GW No.1192 and was withdrawn in 1929.

The third 2-4-0T No.59 *Seaham* built in 1866 and seen here in 1888 (see next photo for subsequent history). (MLS)

Cambrian 2-4-0T GW 1197, formerly Cambrian Railways No.59, built in 1866 and thoroughly overhauled at Swindon between 1922 and 1925, photographed at Oswestry, c1925. It survived on the Tanat Valley branch until 1948, although it had a short spell at Exeter on the Hemyock branch in 1927/8. Both 1196 and 1197 exceeded a million miles in traffic over their 82 year lives.

GWR 824, the former Manning Wardle 0-6-0ST *Mawddwy,* built in 1863, originally named *Alyn,* and sold in 1867 to the Cemmes Road-Dinas Mawddwy light railway, reboilered in 1893 and seen here at Oswestry in 1936. It was numbered No.30 and taken into Cambrian stock in 1913, only being withdrawn in September 1940.

Cambrian Railways No.3, an 0-4-4T built for the Wrexham-Ellesmere branch in 1895. Originally designed by Nasmyth, Wilson & Co. as a 4-4-0T, the Cambrian Locomotive Engineer, Aston, altered it to the 0-4-4T arrangement. With 160lb psi boiler pressure, and two inside 17x24in cylinders, it produced a tractive effort of nearly 15,000 lbs, and was subsequently stationed at Penmaenpool for working between Barmouth and Dolgelley to connect with the GWR there. It survived the GWR amalgamation and was withdrawn in 1932.

Cambrian 0-4-4T No.7, built in 1895 for the Wrexham-Ellesmere branch. It also worked the Llanfyllin branch and at one stage operated over the Llanidloes Mid-Wales line during alterations to the turntable there. It was sent to Swindon for repair in September 1922 but was found to be in poor condition and was condemned. It is seen here, with rail motor trailer No.25, at Oswestry, c1910.

Former Lambourne Valley Railway 0-6-0T *Ealhswith* built by Chapman & Furneaux of Gateshead in 1898, one of three purchased by the Cambrian Railways in June 1904 for £2,000. It had 12x20in cylinders, 3ft 7in diameter wheels, 150 lb boiler pressure and weighed 23 tons 10 cwt. It was photographed at Newbury, c1900, before purchase, with 1898 built Brown Marshall rolling stock. It was renumbered by the Cambrian Railways as No.26. This locomotive took the number of a scrapped engine, and was later renumbered 820 by the GWR, being sold to Mells Collieries near Frome in March 1931. It was broken up by George Cohen's at Wood Lane in 1945. (MLS/F. Moore)

No.26 and its two sister engines (Nos 24 and 35) worked several of the Cambrian branches to Kerry, Llangynog, the Van Valley, Porthywaen and Nantmawr. When photographed shortly after purchase in 1904, it was still painted in the LVR livery of dark blue with black and white lining.

Former Lambourne Valley Railway Hunslet 0-6-0T No.24, purchased by the Cambrian Railways in 1903, 'Swindonised' by the GWR in 1925 and working from Oswestry and Moat Lane on the Van branch until withdrawn in 1946. It is photographed here outshopped from Oswestry Works in the 1930s.

Former Lambourne Valley Railway No.26, purchased by the Cambrian Railways in 1903 and sold by the GWR to Mells Colliery – here at that location, 13 August 1938. (F.K. Davies/J. Hodge Collection)

0-6-0T No.13, built by Sharp, Stewart in 1875 for banking trains from Machynlleth to Talerddig summit – it was in fact initially named *Talerddig* (removed in 1892). It had 4ft 6in diameter wheels, 120lb psi boiler and produced a tractive effort of 13,101 lbs. It remained at Machynlleth until the early 1890s by which time train loads required a more powerful banker and it was transferred to Oswestry for yard shunting. After withdrawal in 1920, it become a stationary boiler at Aberystwyth, although parts of its motion were used to drive machinery in Oswestry Works. The photo was taken around 1900 at Oswestry.

1865 built 2-4-0 No.44 *Rheidol*, which was placed to store in 1906 and, with No.56, was converted in 1907 at Oswestry Works to a 2-4-0 side tank locomotive for auto-working stopping passenger trains between Machynlleth, Aberystwyth and Barmouth. The frames were extended to hold cab and bunker, but the engine was otherwise unaltered. It was withdrawn in July 1922.

GALLERY OF PHOTOS OF OSWESTRY WORKS IN CAMBRIAN AND GWR DAYS

The National Library of Wales has kindly allowed us to show the following photographs which give an idea of the environment within Oswestry Works, most around 1910. It also shows the type of work being undertaken, the equipment available at that time and the rather formal appearance of the workforce. Modern day HSE inspectors might express concerns!

General layout of the Works.

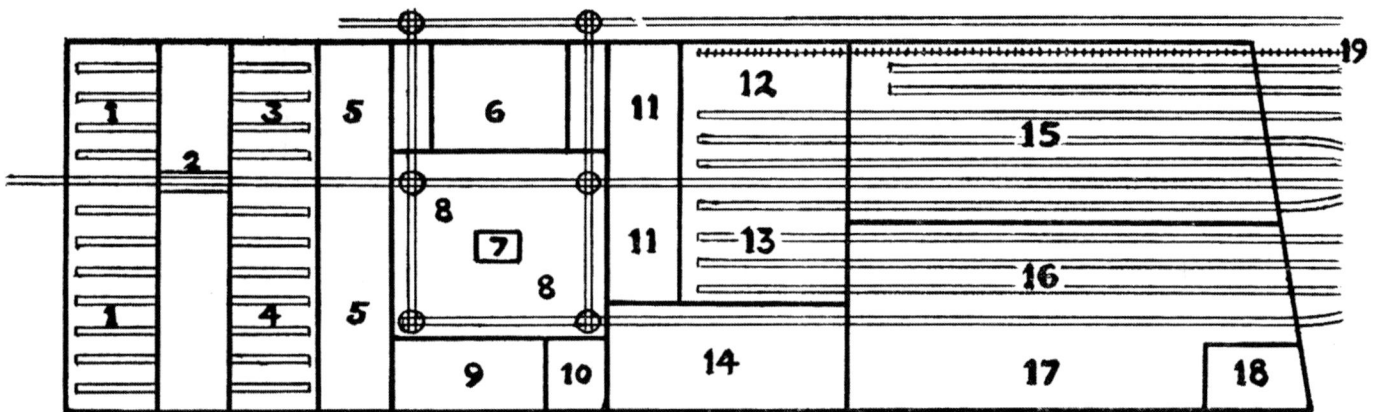

OSWESTRY WORKS

1	Locomotive erecting shop	11	Smithy
2	Traverser	12	Carriage machine shop
3	Tender shop	13	Carriage building shop
4	Boiler shop	14	Foundry
5	Locomotive machine shop	15	Wagon shop
6	Stores with offices over	16	Paint shop
7	Wash-houses and WCs	17	Grease shop
8	Open yard	18	Sheet room
9	Boiler house	19	2 ft gauge tramway to timber drying
10	Brass foundry		

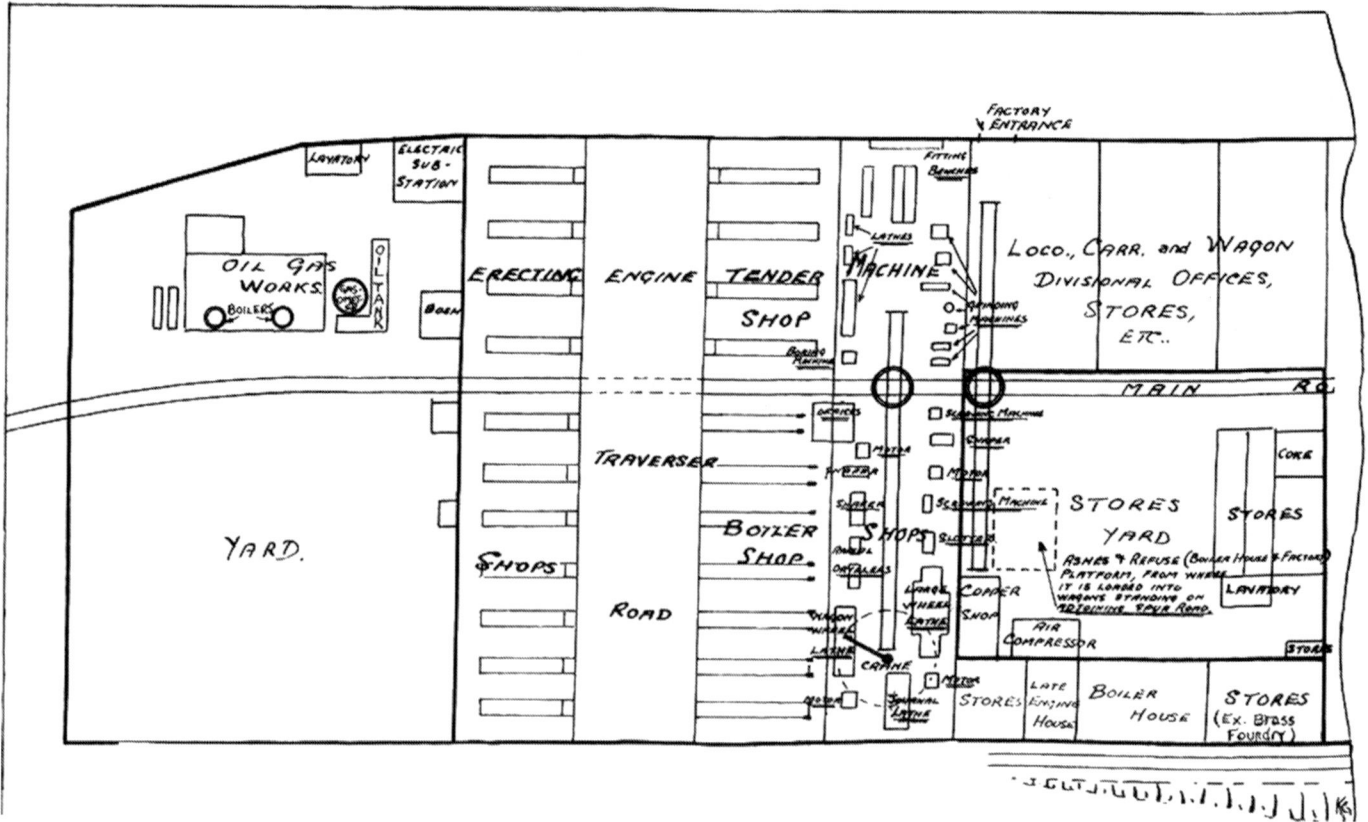

Locomotive Machine and Erecting Shops.

Carriage & Wagon Shops.

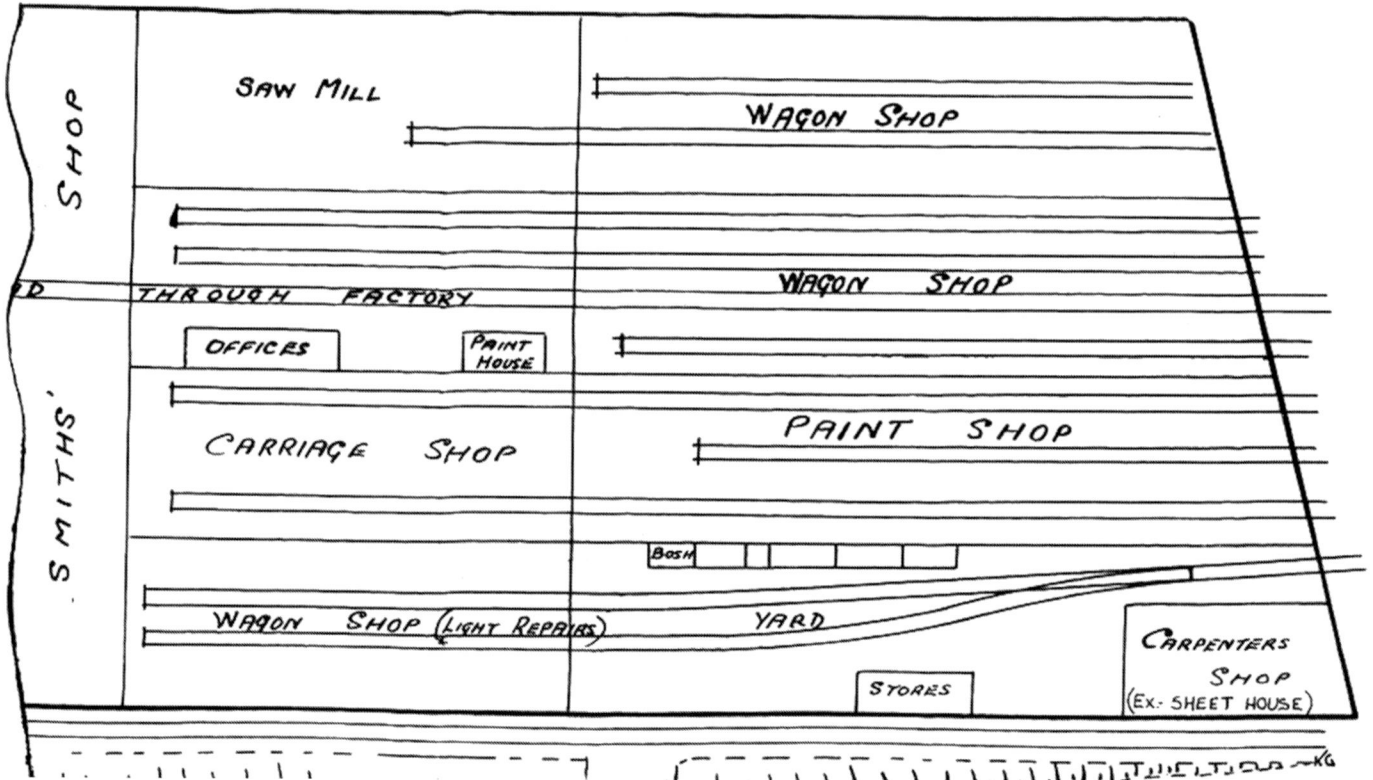

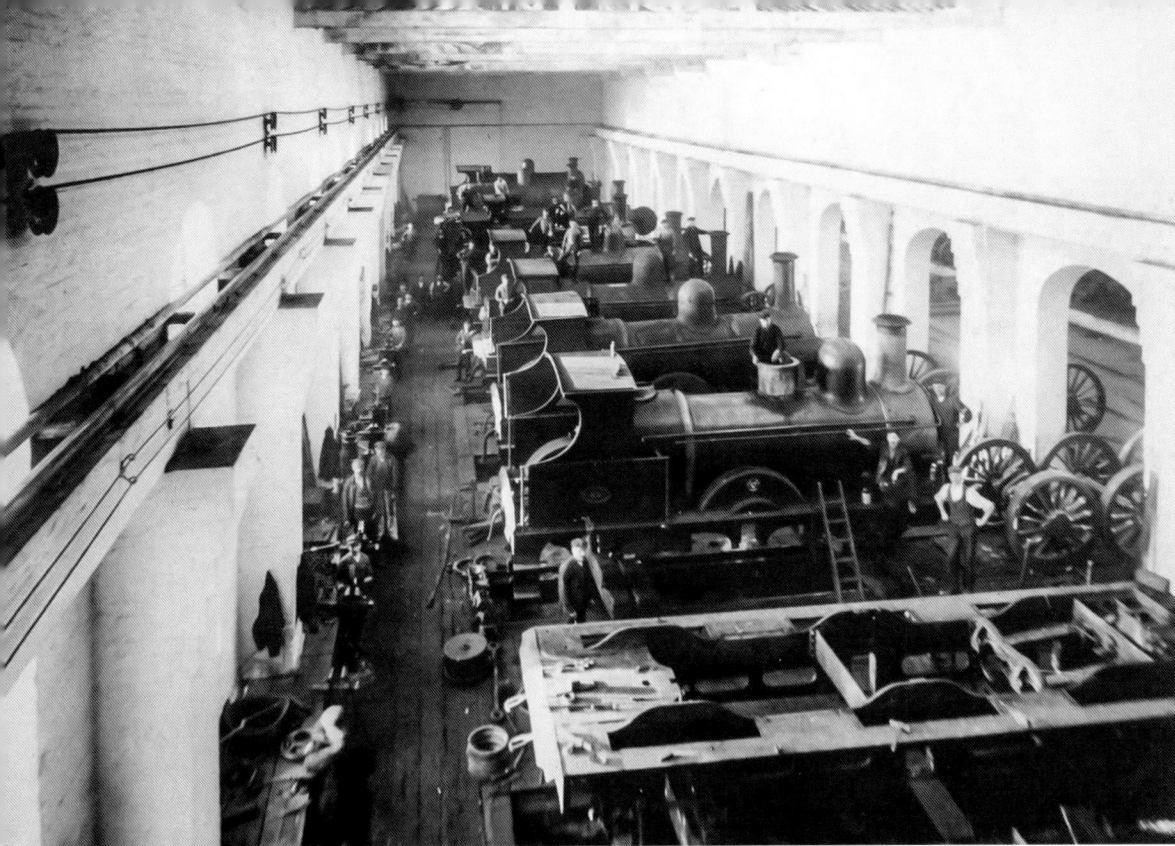

Erecting shop.

Erecting Shop &
workforce.

Tender Section.

Traverser engine.

Carriage Works.

Wagon Section.

Wagon Section.

Wheel Shop.

Wheel drop.

Wheel turning.

Boiler Shop.

Boiler House.

Blacksmiths.

Forge.

Machine Shop.

Foundry.

Drawing Office.

Fitters & Apprentices.

Fitters repairing loco parts.

Axlebox refurbishment of Cambrian 0-6-0 No.875 in the GWR era.

'Dukedog' 9026 in Oswestry Works for overhaul, c1947. (Andrew Dyke collection)

The two Welshpool and Llanfair narrow-gauge engines 822 *The Earl* and 823 *The Countess*, built by Beyer, Peacock for the W&L section of the Cambrian Railways in 1902, stored at Oswestry Works after the closure of the railway in 1956 and before restoration in 1963 when the line was reopened as a 'preserved' line. (Andrew Dyke collection)

A TOUR AROUND THE CAMBRIAN RAILWAYS LANDSCAPE

The authors were offered access to Andrew Dyke's huge collection of photographs of the Cambrian Railways system, many of which have been coloured by Andrew with a technique enabled by digital systems Andrew calls 'colourisation'. This technique has enabled many photos to appear as coloured photographic images even though taken of trains before colour films were widely used by railway photographers of the period. In looking through the collection, the authors were struck by the beautiful landscapes of the Cambrian Railways enhanced by such colourisation, and offer now a tour, as if the reader were a passenger on the *Cambrian Radio Cruise* trains that ran day circular trips for tourists in the 1950s and early 1960s. We therefore complete our 'gallery' of the Cambrian Railways with a round trip by photographs from Crewe (we have 'running powers' from Crewe to Whitchurch), via Oswestry, Newtown and the Mid-Wales line, Machynlleth, Barmouth, Pwllheli and back to Dolgelley.

The coloured photos are augmented by black and white images from Andrew's albums, Bob Miller's Manchester Locomotive Society collection, some colour and black and white photos from Bruce Oliver, and a few from other MLS sources and the Great Western Trust.

We finish our tour of the Cambrian lines at this point and go back for a trip on the iconic train of the company and its successors, the *Cambrian Coast Express*.

We therefore illustrate the journey, as if on the *Cambrian Radio Cruise*, a tourist train of the 1950s and '60s equipped with radio commentary, and always hauled by a BR Standard locomotive as its route included the North Wales coast under LMR patronage. Our route diverts from the Radio Cruise circuit from time to time and we return on the Barmouth-Ruabon Cambrian section of the line as far as Dolgelley instead of along the North Wales coast. The Radio Cruise train is headed in this photograph by BR standard '4' 4-6-0, 75053, which is near Talybont station on the coastal section between Barmouth and Harlech, 1961. (Andrew Dyke colourisation/Rail on Line)

We start our journey in Crewe North locomotive shed in Cambrian Railways times, 1917. 'Large Bogie' 4-4-0 No.47 was built by R. Stephenson & Co. in December 1897. (MLS/R.W. Miller collection/ W.H. Whitworth)

A 'Large Belpaire Goods' 0-6-0, No.92, built in May 1903, at Crewe on a passenger train for Whitchurch and Oswestry, c1912. (MLS/R.W. Miller collection/W.H. Whitworth)

'Large Belpaire'
4-4-0, No.94, at
Crewe station after
reboilering in 1920.
(MLS/R.W. Miller collection/
W.H. Whitworth)

We commence
our Cambrian
journey proper at
Whitchurch station
on the line from
Crewe to Shrewsbury
and Oswestry, the
Cambrian system
starting at this point.
We are standing on
the up platform,
looking towards
Nantwich and
Crewe. (Andrew Dyke
collection)

Whitchurch station with Churchward mogul 5351 on a Crewe-Oswestry freight passing 'Dukedog' 9002 stabled awaiting its next turn, c1955. (MLS)

'Dukedog' 9004 stops at Ellesmere with a Whitchurch-Oswestry train, 19 July 1954. (GW Trust)

Collett 0-6-0
No.2237 arrives
at Ellesmere with
an early afternoon
Whitchurch-
Oswestry train, the
fireman collecting
the token for the
next section, while
a GW 57XX pannier
tank shunts the
goods yard before
continuing with its
pick-up goods train.
(Andrew Dyke colourisation/
Rail on Line)

Collett 0-6-0 2237 on the Cambrian Ellesmere –
Oswestry section with a local Whitchurch-Oswestry
train, 14 February 1957. (MLS/N. Harrop)

The Ellesmere-Wrexham auto train at Bangor-on-Dee, powered by Collett 0-4-2T, 1458, c1958. (Kerry Park)

Collett 57XX 3770 at Sesswick Halt on the 7.40am Wrexham-Ellesmere, June 1961.
(Nick Lera)

Collett 0-4-2T 1432 arrives to pick up the waiting passengers at Hightown Halt, just outside Wrexham on the Wrexham-Ellesmere branch, c1960.
(Andrew Dyke collection)

Wrexham Central station in the 1950s, the photograph taken from the roof of St Giles Church. An auto train for Ellesmere is setting off behind a GW 14XX 0-4-2T. (John Phillips)

A closer view of Wrexham Central station with an LMR train for Wrexham General, headed by a Stanier 3MT 2-6-2T, c1958. (John Phillips)

Oswestry station looking to the north-west, taken from a shelf bank overlooking the town. A train is just departing towards Welshpool, 1 April 1955. (Andrew Dyke colourisation/National Library of Wales)

GWR 'Duke' No.3256 *Guinevere,* built in 1895, double-heading Cambrian 'Large Belpaire' 4-4-0 1014 of 1904 on a freight, at Oswestry, c1925. The 'Dukes' took over much of the Whitchurch-Aberystwyth main line work from the Cambrian engines when the 4-4-0s were scrapped in the mid/late 1920s. (GW Trust)

Cambrian Railways No.37, former
'Met Tank' No. 66, 4-4-0T at
Oswestry with a local freight, c1905.
(MLS/R.W. Miller collection)

GW 0-4-2T No.574 ('517' class) shunting the goods shed at Oswestry,
28 August 1926. (MLS/R.W. Miller collection/H.C. Casserley)

A train of evacuees arrives at Oswestry, transporting children from the Merseyside and Manchester areas at risk of bombardment in the Second World War. The Cambrian lines of the GWR received much wartime traffic, from the evacuees to soldiers at many of the training camps in the Welsh hills. (National Library of Wales)

The circus arrives in Oswestry – schoolchildren mass to watch the arrival of the circus train, congregating in the forecourt of Oswestry station as the elephants are led out into the street, 1 April 1954. (National Library of Wales)

'Dukedog' 9016 at Oswestry with a Whitchurch-Aberystwyth train, the former Cambrian Railways HQ in the background, 1950. (Andrew Dyke colourisation)

Oswestry station with GW passenger pannier tank 6419 in the bay with the auto train for Gobowen whilst a Swindon built Ivatt 2MT 2-6-0 has just arrived in the platform with the 3.5pm Llanfyllin branch train, 30 May 1961. (Andrew Dyke colourisation)

Colourised BYRD

GW passenger pannier tank 5405 and the 11.43am to Gobowen auto train standing at Oswestry's main platform under the Cambrian Railways headquarters. The pannier tank still shows the GWR insignia despite it being several years after nationalisation, 7 May 1953. (Andrew Dyke colourisation)

7802 *Bradley Manor*, one of the earliest regular Cambrian Railways allocated GW 'Manors', with the 5.35pm train to Machynlleth, 4 September 1960. (MLS/R.W. Miller collection)

Llynclys Junction signal box and the branch to Llangynog in the Tanat Valley in 1904, when the Cambrian signals were still in evidence. (Kidderminster Railway Museum Trust)

Sharp, Stewart 0-6-0 No.15 (formerly named *Glansevern*) hauls a two-coach local tender-first on the Llanfyllin branch, at Llanymynech, c1904. (MLS)

No.58 *Gladys* on a Tanat Valley train to Llangynog at Blodwell in 1904 shortly after the opening of that line. (MLS)

GW 1197, ex-Cambrian Railways No.59 *Seaham,* entering Llangedwyn with a Tanat Valley branch train, 20 August 1936. (MLS/R.W. Miller collection)

GW 1197, ex-Cambrian Railways No.59 *Seaham,* at Oswestry with the Tanat Valley branch train, 21 June 1938. (MLS/R.W. Miller collection/ R.J. Buckley)

1197 in its final year of working the Tanat Valley branch, on the 5.25pm Oswestry to Llangynog, 10 May 1947. (MLS/R.W. Miller collection)

A 'Dean Goods', No.2449, is bringing down a ballast train from the quarry in the Tanat Valley, back to Blodwell Junction, Porthywaen and Oswestry, c1953. (Andrew Dyke colourisation/National Library of Wales)

Blodwell Junction on the Tanat Valley line. (Andrew Dyke collection)

2-4-0T 1196 (formerly No. 58 *Gladys*) takes water at Llangynog at the terminus of the Tanat Valley line before returning to Oswestry, 5 July 1941. (Andrew Dyke collection)

Cambrian 'Small Goods' No.898 (Cambrian Railways No.14 built by Sharp, Stewart in 1875), shunts Nantmawr Sidings in the Tanat Valley, 7 May 1935. (Andrew Dyke collection)

7818 *Granville Manor* working a two-coach Welshpool-Oswestry train at Llanymynech, 6 January 1962. (MLS/A.C. Gilbert)

Llanfyllin station and Goods Shed, c1958. (Andrew Dyke collection)

Ivatt 2MT mogul, 46515, built at Swindon, waiting to depart from Llanfyllin with a train for Oswestry, July 1963. (Bruce Oliver)

'Large Belpaire Goods' No. 102, with a passenger train with through coaches to the Great Central Railway, thought to be at Aberystwyth station, August 1921. (MLS/J.M. Bentley)

Pool Quay station, looking north towards Oswestry, the initial terminal point of the Oswestry & Newtown Railway in 1861, where great celebrations were held with much feasting, toasting and the running of an overcrowded inaugural train. (Andrew Dyke collection)

The frontage of Welshpool station in the 1950s with the local bus service competitor to the narrow-gauge Welshpool & Llanfair Railway. (Andrew Dyke collection)

7822 *Foxcote Manor* at Welshpool with a stopping service for Machynlleth and Aberystwyth, 6 April 1963. (MLS/N. Harrop)

Welshpool & Llanfair narrow gauge engine 822 *The Earl* sneaks through the back streets of Welshpool en route to Llanfair Caereinion with an engineer's train. The 2ft 6in line was authorised after the passing of the Light Railways Act in 1896 and opened in 1903. *The Earl* was one of the original two 0-6-0T locomotives built by Beyer, Peacock. (Andrew Dyke collection)

W&L 823 (formerly named *The Countess*) with a Stephenson Locomotive Society special train at Welshpool. (Andrew Dyke collection)

W&L 822 crossing the road at Welshpool – with an unauthorised passenger? (Andrew Dyke collection)

Operational difficulties on the Welshpool & Llanfair Railway. (Andrew Dyke collection)

W&L 822 brings an engineer's train through the streets of Welshpool. (Andrew Dyke collection)

Montgomery station looking towards Welshpool. The station was opened in 1861 as part of the Oswestry & Newtown Railway opened that year, a mile and a half from the county town. The temporary station was replaced by this structure in 1872, with two platforms and passing loop. (Andrew Dyke collection)

Abermule station looking east towards Montgomery and the junction for the Kerry branch. (Andrew Dyke collection)

'Dean Goods' 0-6-0, 2358, with the branch goods at Kerry, c1938. (Andrew Dyke collection)

Sharp, Stewart 0-4-0ST No.36 *Plasfynnon*, built in 1863, at Kerry with a mixed train, July 1904. No.36 was withdrawn two years later. (MLS/R.W. Miller collection)

No.36 *Plasfynnon* working the mixed branch train to Kerry, c1903. (MLS/R.W.Miller collection)

Newtown station, hub of the initial Cambrian companies – the Llanidloes and Newtown, and the Oswestry and Newtown, which joined together in 1861 and became the Cambrian Railways in 1864. 7821 *Ditcheat Manor* stands ready to depart westwards with a freight, while a Swindon built Ivatt 2MT mogul shunts the goods yard, c1960. (Andrew Dyke collection)

Churchward mogul 6342 enters Newtown station with a Birmingham-Aberystwyth holiday express formed of LMS coaches, c1958. (GW Trust)

7810 *Draycott Manor* with the 12.35pm Aberystwyth-Whitchurch at Moat Lane Junction, while 2MT mogul 46511 sets back from the platform having arrived with the 12.45pm from Builth Wells, 24 October 1962. (MLS)

Cambrian 2-4-0T No.57 *Maglona*, built in 1866, working the Elan Valley branch at Elan Valley Railway Junction, 3 August 1898. It was engaged with the Birmingham Corporation Waterworks construction, based at Llanidloes and after completion of the work, joined its sisters on the Tanat Valley line. It was condemned at Swindon in July 1922, reprieved, renumbered 1192 and worked the Hemyock branch from Exeter until withdrawal in August 1929. (MLS/R.W. Miller collection)

The small loco shed at Llanidloes housing a Swindon built Ivatt 2MT 2-6-0 and one of the last surviving 'Dean Goods' that it and its sisters replaced, 2538, outside the shed. (Andrew Dyke collection)

Cambrian 0-6-0 No.873 at Llanidloes on the
first section of the Cambrian Railways opened
as the Llanidloes and Newtown in 1861, with a
stopping passenger train to Talyllyn Junction and
Brecon over the former Mid-Wales Railway,1947.
(MLS/R.W. Miller collection)

A Brecon-Hereford train near Groesffordd Halt
headed by 'Dean Goods' 0-6-0 No.2354, c1953.
This is a typical formation of trains working from
Brecon on the Mid-Wales line. (Andrew Dyke colourisation)

844 on the 12.45pm to Moat Lane at Builth Wells on the former Mid-Wales Railway, and GW 0-4-2T 5801 on the 1.10pm to Brecon, 15 September 1949. (MLS/R.W. Miller collection/W.A. Camwell)

0-6-0 No.855 near Erwood on a Moat Lane-Brecon train, 10 October 1950. (Andrew Dyke collection)

Cambrian class '15' 0-6-0 No.896 at Newbridge-on-Wye with the 2.40pm Moat Lane-Brecon approaching and at the station, 15 September 1949. (MLS/W.A. Camwell)

Cambrian Railways 0-6-0 No.893, formerly No.99, built by Beyer, Peacock in 1908, at Builth Wells with a freight for Moat Lane, 15 September 1949. (MLS/W.A. Camwell)

2MT mogul 46510 at Three Cocks Junction with a Brecon-Moat Lane and Newtown train, 4 July 1962. (Bruce Oliver)

Ivatt mogul 46527 arrives at Three Cocks Junction with a train for Brecon from Moat Lane, 4 July 1962. (Bruce Oliver)

Collett 0-6-0 2257 with ex-ROD tender, at Talyllyn Junction with the 10.32am
Brecon-Hereford, 22 August 1953. (MLS/J.D. Darby)

Class '73' 0-6-0, No.77, working a passenger train over the former B&M main line near Merthyr, 1922. Shortly after absorption by the GWR, it was renumbered 880 and survived until 1938. (MLS/R.W. Miller collection)

A Churchward 63XX mogul enters Carno station with a morning Machynlleth-Welshpool/Whitchurch stopping train, c1958. (GW Trust)

7828 *Odney Manor* heads the down *Cambrian Coast Express* between Moat Lane and Caersws beside the River Severn, c1961. (Andrew Dyke collection)

Caersws station looking west towards Machynlleth. It is a grade II listed building, constructed in 1864 after the line opened in 1862, and it is one of the few early Cambrian Railways stations that have been preserved. The signal box dates from the same era and was not replaced until an automatic barrier crossing was installed in 2010. (Michael Marshall collection)

BR Standard '4' 4-6-0 75023 and 7819 *Hinton Manor* (deprived of name and number plates) rush over the trestle bridge at Caersws across the River Severn from Machynlleth and Aberystwyth towards Welshpool and Shrewsbury, August 1965.
(Andrew Dyke collection/ Phil Waterfield)

Hunslet 0-6-0T No.819 of 1903, Cambrian Railways No.24, bought by the Cambrian in 1903 from the Lambourne Valley Railway, is seen here with an engineers' train finally dismantling the Van Railway in 1940.
(National Library of Wales)

'Large Belpaire' 4-4-0 No.95 with the 9.5am express from Aberystwyth to Whitchurch on Talerddig bank, assisted in the rear to the summit by '61' class 4-4-0 'Large Bogie' No.72, 15 August 1913. The train engine (No.95) was involved in the head-on collision with '61' class No.82 in the Abermule disaster in January 1921 and both were cut up at the accident site. (MLS/R.W. Miller collection)

7819 *Hinton Manor* (now preserved) nears the summit of Talerddig Bank through the deep rock cutting with the up *Cambrian Coast Express*, c1962. (Andrew Dyke collection)

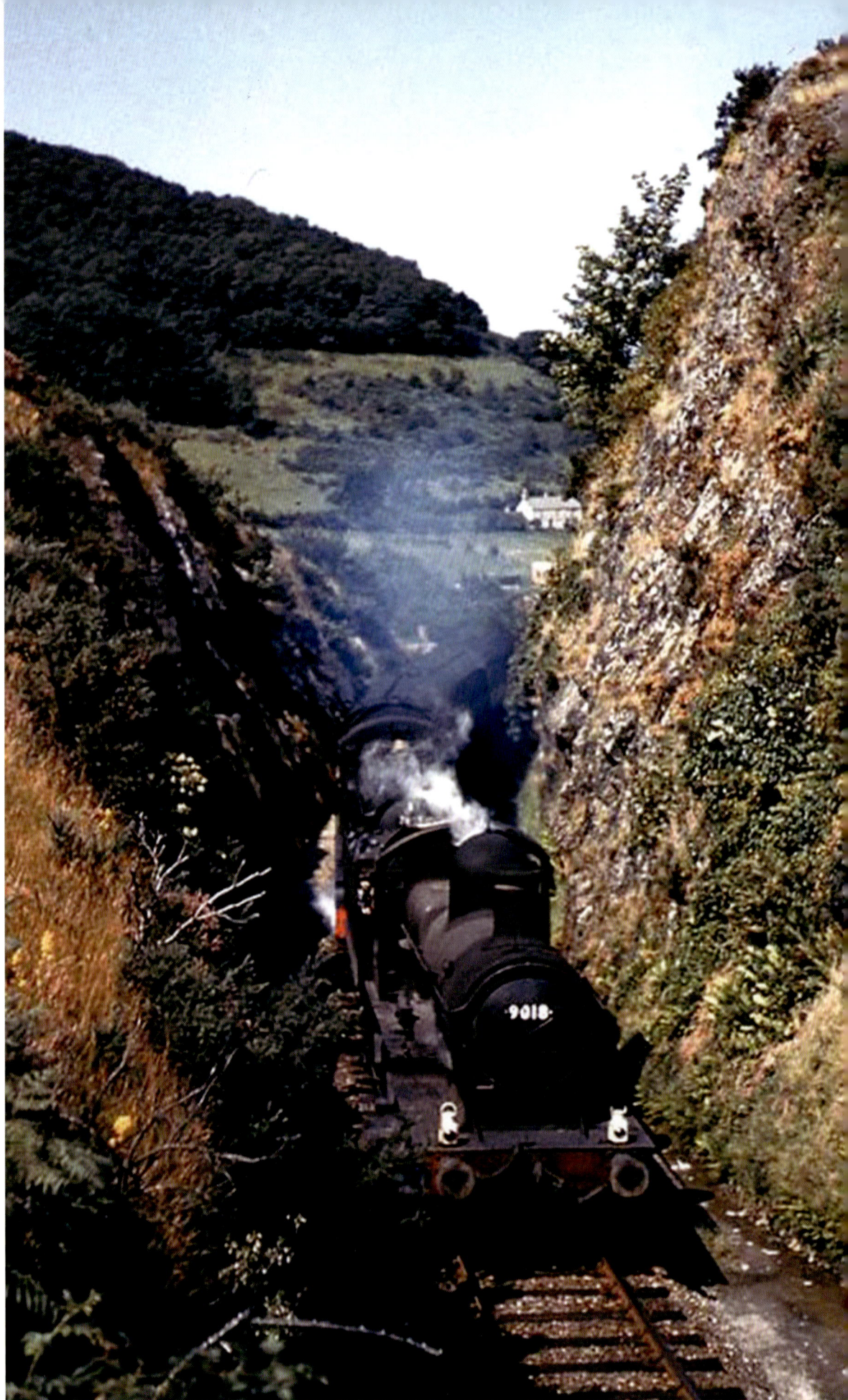

'Dukedog'
9018 assists
7803 *Barcote
Manor* in the final
stages of the
climb to Talerddig
summit with an
Aberystwyth-
Birmingham holiday
express, c1955.
(Andrew Dyke collection)

A BR Standard 4 2-6-4T enters Talerddig station with a Machynlleth – Moat Lane Junction train, c1963. (GW Trust)

A Churchward 63XX mogul with steam to spare drags a long freight up to Talerddig summit banked by a Swindon built Ivatt 2MT 2-6-0, c1960. (Andrew Dyke colourisation)

7807 *Compton Manor* struggles to the summit of Talerddig with an eastbound train in the harsh winter snow of early 1963. (Colour-Rail)

7810 *Draycott Manor* leads the down *Cambrian Coast Express* past Commins Coch Halt and over the Afon Twymyn, on the descent from Talerddig through Llanbrynmair to Machynlleth, 1961. (Andrew Dyke collection)

Cemmes Road station and signal box with the signalman holding the single-line token for the next westbound train for Machynlleth and the coast. (Andrew Dyke collection)

Dinas Mawddwy terminus and goods shed.
(Andrew Dyke collection)

Sharp, Stewart 2-4-0 No.53, formerly named *Gladstone,* built in October 1865 for the Cambrian Railways after its formation, approaches Machynlleth with the 8.30am branch train from Dinas Mawddwy, 15 August 1913. (MLS/R.W. Miller collection)

7827 *Lydham Manor* and 7819 *Hinton Manor* double-head the Ffestiniog Railway AGM special at Machynlleth, 20 April 1963. (MLS)

An aerial view of Machynlleth station and surrounding countryside looking toward the coast, with a Pwllheli-Welshpool-Shrewsbury stopping train headed by a BR Standard '4' 4-6-0 entering the station. (Andrew Dyke collection)

Sharp, Stewart 2-4-0 No.43, originally named *Plynlimon*, rebuilt by Aston in 1892, at Machynlleth shed, 2 July 1909, allocated GW No. 1331 but the number was never carried, and the engine was withdrawn in July 1922. (MLS/R.W. Miller collection)

Former Cambrian Railways 0-6-0 No.15 built in 1918, which survived as BR Western Region No.844 until August 1954, at Machynlleth shed, 19 July 1953. (MLS)

Three generations of Cambrian motive power in GWR days standing ready at Machynlleth shed, 'Dukedog' 9017 based on the original Dean small-wheeled 4-4-0s, Churchward mogul 6392 and Collett 0-6-0 2298, c1960. (Andrew Dyke colourisation/ Rail on Line)

The successor to the Cambrian 4-4-0s, the GW 'Dukes' and 'Dukedogs', BR Standard '2' 2-6-0 No.78000 in BR black livery at Machynlleth shed, 15 June 1958. (MLS)

2-4-0 No.41 at Machynlleth with the 6.10pm train to Pwllheli, 14 August 1913. (MLS/R.W. Miller collection)

Aston's class '73' 0-6-0 of 1894, No.884 (formerly Cambrian Railways No.87 built in January 1899 by Neilson, Reid & Co.) at Machynlleth with a train for Barmouth, c1930. 884 survived until just before nationalisation, being condemned in August 1947. (MLS/R.W.Miller collection)

3259 *Merlin,* one of the Machynlleth allocation of 'Dukes' in the 1920s, standing at Machynlleth station with a stopping train for Newtown and Welshpool, the driver being handed the token for the section to Cemmes Road, c1929. (GW Trust)

The remote wilderness of Dovey Junction with the line to Barmouth and Pwllheli curving off to the right, while a train from Aberystwyth to Machynlleth headed by a BR Standard '4' 4-6-0 departs eastbound from the station. (Andrew Dyke collection/T.B. Owen)

Collett 0-6-0 2202 on the left with a train from Pwllheli and 7807 *Compton Manor* on the right with an Aberystwyth-Shrewsbury train connect at Dovey Junction, 31 May 1960. (Colour-Rail/L.V.Reason)

7819 *Hinton Manor* departs from Ynyslas station and crosses the small trestle bridge over the Afon Leri, c1963. (Andrew Dyke collection)

Cambrian Railways 0-4-4T, GWR No.19, formerly Cambrian Railways No.8, which received heavy repairs at Swindon in between 1922 and 1925 and received GW chimney, smokebox, safety valves and GW pattern bunker. It was renumbered by the GWR as No.19, and was allocated to Machynlleth, working trains to Pwllheli. In 1927 it was transferred to Aberystwyth where it and surviving sister, No.10, (ex-No.3) performed station shunting duties and the occasional local passenger train to Machynlleth. It is seen here at Aberystwyth performing station pilot duties, 1930. (MLS/R.W. Miller collection)

Cambrian Railways 0-4-4T, No.8, built in 1895 for the Wrexham-Ellesmere branch, at Plascrug Crossing, Aberystwyth, with a local passenger train from Machynlleth, c1920. (MLS/R.W. Miller collection)

'Large Bogie' No.67, built in May 1893, approaching Aberystwyth with a train from Whitchurch, September 1921. No.67 was withdrawn in July 1930. (MLS/R.W. Miller collection)

7819 *Hinton Manor* ready to depart from Aberystwyth with the *Cambrian Coast Express,* a BR Standard '4' tank waiting to follow with a stopping train to Machynlleth, and far left, a Collett 22XX 0-6-0 on a train to Carmarthen, c1962. (John Maudsley)

Collett 0-6-0 2217 arrives at Aberystwyth with a train from Carmarthen and Lampeter, 6 July 1962. (Bruce Oliver)

A Churchward mogul has arrived at Aberystwyth with the newly overhauled Vale of Rheidol narrow gauge engine, No.9 *Prince of Wales,* while No.7 *Owain Glyndwr* waits on the narrow-gauge track with an engineer's train, c1960. The Cambrian Railways took over the line in 1913. It was the only BR steam operated line between 1968 and 1989 when it was privatised. (Rail on Line)

Whilst in Aberystwyth, we visit the Cambrian narrow-gauge Vale of Rheidol railway, a 1ft 11¾in gauge line built independently in 1902 and absorbed by the Cambrian Railways in 1913. One of the three locomotives, No. 7 *Owain Glyndwr*, built by the GWR in 1923, leaves the Aberystwyth narrow-gauge terminus, 1963. (Andrew Dyke collection)

No.9 *Prince of Wales,* a GWR 1924 rebuild of the original V of R No.2, renumbered 1213 by the GW in 1923, climbs into the hills on the tortuous route from Aberystwyth to Devil's Bridge, 1961. (Andrew Dyke collection)

Collett 0-6-0 2200 with an Aberystwyth-Dovey Junction train at Bow Street, c1960. (GW Trust)

Glandyfi station just north of the Dovey Estuary on the line from Dovey Junction to Barmouth and Pwllheli. A northbound train for Barmouth headed by a BR Standard 3MT 2-6-2T 82000 class is passed by a southbound train hauled by a BR Standard 4MT 2-6-4T, c1965. (Andrew Dyke collection)

Collett 0-6-0 3208 with a Machynlleth – Pwllheli train at Abertafol Halt between Glandyfi and Aberdovey, c1960. (GW Trust)

BR Std 3 2-6-2T 82033 at Penhelig Halt with a Pwllheli – Machynlleth train, c1963. (GW Trust)

Small Goods No.14 (formerly named *Broneirion*) shunting wagons on the Harbour branch at Aberdovey Quay, 16 July 1912. (MLS/R.W. Miller collection/H.W. Burman)

Vulcan Foundry class '73' 0-6-0, No.78, built in 1895, at Machynlleth, 28 June 1909. It was fitted with a superheated boiler by the GW in 1924 and received the number 881, being withdrawn in 1932. It was photographed shunting wagons on the Harbour branch at Aberdovey, c1911. (MLS/R.W. Miller collection)

'Large Belpaire Goods' 0-6-0, No.91, one of the class '15' goods engines introduced in 1903 by the Locomotive Superintendent, Mr Jones, who followed Aston. It is shunting on Aberdovey Quay c1911 and was allocated GW No.889 but this was never carried as the engine was withdrawn in August 1922. (MLS/R.W. Miller collection)

A Swindon built Ivatt 2MT 2-6-0 shunts a freight down among the sand dunes on the old Aberdovey Quay branch, c1958. (Kidderminster Railway Museum Trust)

No.36, rebuilt 4-4-0 'Met Tank', on a Machynlleth-Barmouth local between Aberdovey and Towyn, c1920. (MLS/R.W. Miller collection/H.W. Burman)

Class '15' Goods No.895 at Towyn with a Pwllheli-Machynlleth stopping train, 1953. (MLS/P. Ward)

'Dukedog' 9014 arrives at Towyn with a Machynlleth – Pwllheli stopping train, while *Sir Haydn* of the Talyllyn Railway poses on the left, c1956. (Andrew Dyke collection)

Llwyngwril signal box standing isolated on the northbound platform with a view out to sea with the Dovey Estuary on the left. The small signal box of Cambrian Railways origin housed thirteen levers and was redundant when the loop was removed. (Andrew Dyke colourisation)

2264 enters Llwyngwril station with the 3.25pm Barmouth to Dovey Junction stopping train, to connect there with an Aberystwyth-Machynlleth service, 2 August 1955. (Andrew Dyke colourisation)

BR Standard '4' 4-6-0 75002 clambers up to the Friog cliff snow shelter with a southbound freight with a glorious view of Fairbourne and the Mawddach Estuary as backdrop, c1965. (Andrew Dyke collection)

82003 blows off steam furiously as it waits to depart from Fairbourne station with the 3.40pm local train from Machynlleth to Pwllheli, 29 July 1964. The Friog cliffs form the backdrop and a camper coach is in the siding. (Geoff Plumb)

'Small Bogie' No.21 'built in 1886' comes off Barmouth bridge into Barmouth Junction with a train for Machynlleth, c1911. (MLS/R.W. Miller collection)

Cambrian Railways 0-6-0 No.884 at Barmouth Junction with a freight, c1925.
(MLS/R.W. Miller collection/A.G. Ellis)

A Collett '2251' class 0-6-0 with a freight off the Ruabon/Dolgelley route at Barmouth Junction, c1960. (GW Trust)

A 22XX Collett 0-6-0 approaches Barmouth Junction with a train for Dolgelley and Ruabon, c1957. (Andrew Dyke collection)

Class '15' 0-6-0 894 (Cambrian No.100) rumbles across Barmouth Bridge with a northbound freight, c1952. (Andrew Dyke collection)

A Collett 22XX 0-6-0 draws a freight across Barmouth bridge on a glorious sunny day with the 2,900 ft Cader Idris looming on the skyline, c1958. (Andrew Dyke collection)

A spectacular sunset over Cader Idris as a BR Standard '4' 4-6-0 meanders slowly southwards over Barmouth Bridge, the estuary exposed by the receding tide, c1965. (Andrew Dyke collection)

2-4-0 No.28, formerly *Mazeppa*, running into Barmouth with a train from Welshpool and Machynlleth, c1895. (MLS/R.W. Miller collection)

'Dukedog' 9005 runs light engine towards Barmouth station over the wooden trestle Old Chapel Bridge just before it was rebuilt using concrete instead of wood, 21 August 1951. (MLS/N. Fields)

A 73XX Churchward mogul on the rebuilt Old Chapel Bridge at Barmouth, with a Dolgelley-Barmouth local train, 1952. (Andrew Dyke collection/Derek Cross)

Cambrian 4-4-0, No.1091, at Barmouth at the head of a train for Machynlleth, c1923. (MLS/R.W. Miller collection)

'Dukedog' 9020 leaving Barmouth with a stopping train to Machynlleth, just before it reaches Barmouth Bridge, c1955. (GW Trust)

7825 *Lechlade Manor* leaving Barmouth with a Barmouth-Chester via Bala and Ruabon train, 21 August 1951. (MLS)

Collett goods 0-6-0 2270 leaving Barmouth with a train for Birkenhead via Dolgelley, Bala and Ruabon, 30 August 1937. (MLS)

We now make a pause on our 'cruise'. BR Standard '4' 4-6-0 75034 on the *Cambrian Radio Cruise* train is at Barmouth on the northbound run, 1 August 1961. Initially 75020 and 75026 were allocated to this duty, then later more Standards were available as they replaced 'Manors' on the normal service trains. (MLS)

A busy scene at Barmouth station as a BR Standard 3MT 2-6-2T shunts in the goods yard, two trains occupy the through platforms, a two-coach local hauled by an Ivatt 2MT mogul has arrived in the bay and a BR Standard '4' 2-6-4T assembles stock in the carriage sidings, the whole scene framed by the Cader Idris range of mountains, still glistening from a recent squall of rain. (Andrew Dyke collection)

'Small Goods' 0-6-0, No.45, formerly named *Rhiewport*, with a down goods between Llanbedr and Pensarn, c1911. This engine outlived its sisters by a considerable margin, not being withdrawn until September 1945. (MLS/R.W. Miller collection)

4-4-0 No.17 departing from Llanbedr with a local train for Harlech, Portmadoc and Pwllheli, 25 July 1911. No.17 was built in 1878 and reboilered in March 1911. It was renumbered 1116 in 1922 and withdrawn in September 1924. (MLS/R.W. Miller collection)

4-4-0 No.16 *Beaconsfield*, de-named and fitted with replacement boiler, on a coastal section train near Llandanwg, c1913. (MLS/R.W. Miller collection)

'Small Goods' 0-6-0 No.10 (formerly named *Marchioness*) on an up coastal goods train between Harlech and Llandanwg, 26 July 1911. (MLS/R.W. Miller collection/H.W. Burman)

Sharp, Stewart 2-4-0 No. 28 leaving Harlech with a train for Machynlleth, c1911. (MLS/R.W. Miller collection)

No.41, Sharp, Stewart 2-4-0, formerly named *Countess Vane,* with an up freight near Harlech, c1911. (MLS/R.W. Miller collection)

'Duke' 3254 *Cornubia* of 1895 heads a freight northbound photographed from the ramparts of Harlech Castle high above. (Andrew Dyke collection)

Small Bogie 4-4-0 No.20, built by Sharp, Stewart & Co. in 1886, accelerates a stopping train under the cliffs at Harlech towards Portmadoc and Pwllheli, c1911. (MLS/R.W. Miller collection)

A Pwllheli-Machynlleth local train hauled by a hard-working 'Dukedog' 9025, between Penrhyndeudraeth and Talsarnau, c1956. (Andrew Dyke colourisation/Rail on Line)

Cambrian 'Small Goods' 0-6-0, formerly No.48 built in 1873, reboilered in 1889, and released from Oswestry Works in 1923 after repair following a GW decision not to withdraw, at Portmadoc with a freight train, c1924. (MLS/R.W. Miller collection)

Ivatt 2MT 2-6-0 46509 stands at Portmadoc station with the 12.45pm Pwllheli-Barmouth, waiting for the crossing gates to open, 8 August 1964. (Geoff Plumb)

We are now in the slate area of Portmadoc and the Ffestiniog Railway and still find a horse-drawn slate train that would have predated the coming of the railways in this part of the world. (Andrew Dyke colourisation/ National Library of Wales)

The Cambrian Railways' 0-6-0 goods successor, the GW Collett '2251' class, No.2233 at Criccieth, 1960. (MLS/G.A. Coltas)

A BR Standard 3MT 2-6-2T steams past Criccieth Castle with a Pwllheli-Machynlleth train, c1962. The castle was built by Llewelyn the Great, captured by King Edward I and burnt by Owain Glyndwr. (Roger Joanes)

7330, a Collett version of the Churchward mogul with improved cab design, arrives at Afon Wen with a Dovey Junction-Pwllheli train, while 3MT 82009 waits to depart for Barmouth. Spare carriages for relief trains to and from Butlins Holiday Camp can be seen in the sidings, 3 July 1961. (Andrew Dyke collection/L. Rowe)

78007 and a second BR Standard 2MT 2-6-0, at Pwllheli station, 22 May 1956. (Colour-Rail/T. Owen)

BR Standard 3MT 2-6-2T 82000 waiting to depart from Pwllheli with a Machynlleth train, 29 April 1964. (Colour-Rail)

We retrace our steps to Barmouth and the Cambrian branch to Dolgelley where it joined the GWR line to Bala, Llangollen and Ruabon. A 63XX Churchward mogul wanders along the beautiful Mawddach Estuary near Arthog, the station before Barmouth Junction (now Morfa Mawddach), with a train from Ruabon and Dolgelley, c1960. (Andrew Dyke collection)

Cambrian 0-4-4T No. 3 leaving Arthog with a Dolgelley-Pwllheli train, c1920. (MLS/R.W. Miller collection)

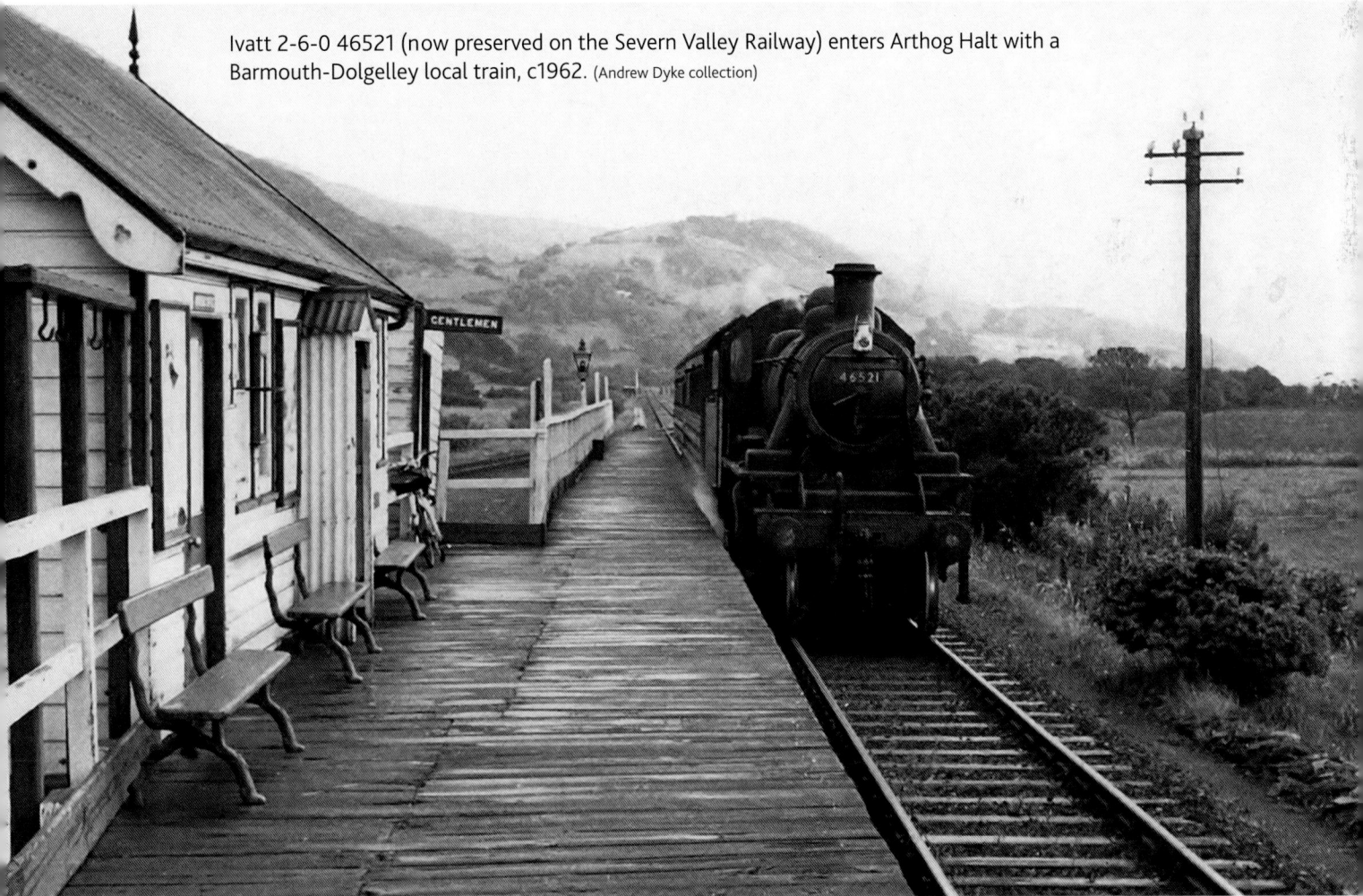

Ivatt 2-6-0 46521 (now preserved on the Severn Valley Railway) enters Arthog Halt with a Barmouth-Dolgelley local train, c1962. (Andrew Dyke collection)

Mogul 6357 enters Arthog Halt with a Ruabon-Barmouth train, c1958. (GW Trust)

Livestock Market Day in Dolgelley in the 1930s when the railway still played a significant part in the movement of livestock, with a flock of Welsh sheep being gathered ready for shipment at the end of the day. (Andrew Dyke collection)

A Collett 22XX 0-6-0 curves round the Mawddach River arriving at Dolgelley from Barmouth with a stopping train for Bala and Ruabon, c1960. (Andrew Dyke collection)

BR Std 2 2-6-0 78006 stands at Dolgelley station with a two-coach shuttle train to Barmouth, c1962. The station building on the left is the GWR structure, on the right, the Cambrian Railways building. (GW Trust)

THE CAMBRIAN COAST EXPRESS

No book about the Cambrian Railways is complete without a reference to the *Cambrian Coast Express,* and therefore a small selection of photos of that train in its origins, heyday and final form are included together with the recollections of that train.

David Maidment's memories of the train

As I was based at Old Oak Common for relief clerical work during my college vacations during 1957 and 1958, my first memories of the *Cambrian Coast Express* are of seeing the Old Oak engines selected for the London-Shrewsbury leg being polished and prepared for the 10.10am Paddington departure, fitted with the chocolate and cream painted impressive headboard. Although this turn was considered by the crews to be the hardest Old Oak turn (out and back, 356 miles, paid well, but tough, especially for the fireman), it was the depot's second best 'Castle' that was regularly rostered (the best was allocated to the *Bristolian*). In 1957, it was 5082 *Swordfish* (on which I cadged a lift back from Paddington to Old Oak when fetching the depot's pay day cash safe) and in the summer of 1958, it was the double-chimneyed 7013 *Bristol Castle* (the former 4082 *Windsor Castle,* identities exchanged for the 1952 royal funeral). This was followed by one of 81A's best 'Castles' in September, 5035 *Coity Castle* (5043 was the *Bristolian* engine). Weekdays it was a lightweight seven or eight coach train, but on summer Saturdays it loaded to ten, twelve or at the peak, thirteen coaches.

In July 1960, as a young student, I joined others holidaying at the Methodist Guild Holiday Home in Barmouth. I took the 9.10am Paddington to Wolverhampton, hauled by 6024 *King Edward I* which delivered its 13-coach train on time. I then alighted and waited for the *Cambrian Coast Express,* on this summer Saturday also a 13-coach train but run from Wolverhampton non-stop to Welshpool avoiding Shrewsbury station by traversing the Abbey Foregate triangle. The train arrived from Paddington 23 minutes late behind 6000 *King George V* and a Shrewsbury engine, 7811 *Dunley Manor,* and a dirty Stourbridge Churchward mogul, 6340, backed on. They set off with great vigour, attaining 73mph by Albrighton before suffering a series of brutal signal checks from a stopping DMU that had been allowed to precede the late running express. After more checks to walking pace at Shifnal, the pair roused the echoes lifting the 500-ton train to 38mph at Hollinswood summit. Yet more checks and the train was 45 minutes late at Shrewsbury, but with some nimble work between collecting the single line tokens, was just 35 minutes late at Welshpool, where the pair were replaced by Machynlleth's gleaming 7818 *Granville Manor* and clean Standard '4', 75026. Despite a four-minute stand just before Moat Lane Junction awaiting an up train, and a minute stand outside Machynlleth, we were 32 minutes late there, where 75026 cut off to allow 7818 to proceed with the Aberystwyth seven coaches. 75026 then continued with the Pwllheli portion arriving somewhat wearily into Barmouth 43 minutes late. I returned to London via Bala and Ruabon on a 10-coach express hauled by a pair of Collett 22XX 0-6-0s (with a 'Grange' from Ruabon and a 'King' from Wolverhampton).

A few years later, in June 1963, when concluding my railway management training in the Cardiff Division, I spent an afternoon travelling between Shrewsbury and Machynlleth on the down *Cambrian Coast Express* with 7828 *Odney Manor*. With just six GW liveried BR Mark 1 coaches, it was easy, early at Welshpool, Newtown and Machynlleth stops. After slowing to 28mph to collect the token at Carno, we accelerated to 35mph before falling to 26mph at Talerddig summit, freewheeling to 67mph on the descent.

A year later, taking an afternoon off from my station master's duties at Aberbeeg, I caught the *CCE* again at Shrewsbury, this time with Machynlleth's favourite 7819 *Hinton Manor*. The train was 20 minutes late arriving (behind a D10XX 'Western' diesel hydraulic), but with just five coaches we knocked four minutes

off the scheduled time to Welshpool (top speed 63mph), regained another six minutes on to Newtown and then disaster struck – a complete token failure at Caersws which lasted nearly an hour. We then roared away attaining 47mph before a walking pace signal check at Carno, then thundered up to Talerddig summit at 47mph, reaching 62mph between braking for curves on the descent. I alighted at Machynlleth and went through to Portmadoc for a trip on the Ffestiniog, behind a 'Standard' on a connecting train, stayed there overnight and caught the up *Cambrian Coast Express* the following morning, with ex-works 7811 *Dunley Manor* on seven coaches. We stopped at Penrhyndeudraeth, Harlech and Barmouth – on time without any concerns this time – before I alighted to return back to South Wales via Bala and Ruabon with 'Standard' 75006 and just three coaches. Thereafter, I sought out 'Manors' on locals between Shrewsbury and Welshpool and did not attempt the *Cambrian Coast Express* after it had 'dumbed down' to maroon coaches and Standard '4' haulage.

The pre-war *Cambrian Coast Express* leaving Aberystwyth for London on the first leg of its journey to Shrewsbury behind 'Duke' 3272 (built in January 1897 as 3281 *Fowey*) and 'Dukedog' 3207 (built in December 1936 as 3207 *Earl of St Germans*), 13 August 1939. 3272 lost its name at the end of the 1920s when the Paddington PR Department felt that such names misled the passengers and was withdrawn in June 1949, numbered 9072. 3207 lost its name to 'Castle' 5050 almost immediately and surprisingly was withdrawn as 9007 in August 1948 before the older engine. (MLS)

7803 *Barcote Manor*, still in BR plain black livery, takes water at Welshpool with the down *Cambrian Coast Express*, formed of 'crimson and cream' liveried GW Hawksworth and Collett rolling stock, c1955. (Andrew Dyke collection)

A difficult photo to date, as the BR Standard pair, 75006 4MT 4-6-0 and 78002 2MT 2-6-0, are from a later era whilst the 'plum & spilt milk' ex-GW coaches are from an earlier period. Some 'Standards' came to the Cambrian in the mid-1950s, so this photo, taken of the up *Cambrian Coast Express* at Machynlleth, must have been taken around 1956, before the train was earmarked for chocolate and cream rolling stock and Brunswick Green 'Manor' haulage in the late 1950s and early 1960s. (Andrew Dyke colourisation/Rail on Line)

Machynlleth shed provided a Collett 0-6-0, No.2285, to work the Pwllheli portion of the *Cambrian Coast Express* instead of the usual 'Manor' or BR Standard '4' 4-6-0, 26 February 1958. The 0-6-0 bears the later chocolate & cream headboard, but still has GW era coaching stock. (MLS)

The same 0-6-0, 2285, returns with the Pwllheli portion of the *Cambrian Coast Express* which it will work as far as Machynlleth, approaching Barmouth Junction, a few months later in 1958. It now has a train of chocolate & cream BR Mark 1 stock, but has the earlier black and silver headboard. (GW Trust)

GW Small Prairie, 5541 of Machynlleth shed, has just arrived at Machynlleth station with the Pwllheli portion of the *Cambrian Coast Express*, which will be amalgamated here with the Aberystwyth portion and its 'Manor' which will take the train forward. 5541 in Brunswick green livery and the train in chocolate and cream are immaculate, c1959. (Andrew Dyke collection)

Machynlleth's 7818 *Granville Manor* leading Collett 0-6-0 2200 which hauled the Pwllheli portion approaching Shrewsbury with the eleven coach up *Cambrian Coast Express* on the last Saturday of the 1960 summer service, 24 September 1960. The eight coach weekday chocolate and cream Mark 1 rake has been strengthened with a maroon Mark 1 at the rear and Collett and Hawksworth maroon coaches at the front. The train will reverse at Shrewsbury. (T.E. Williams)

After reversal, Stafford Road's 5059 *Earl St. Aldwyn* accelerates hard from Shrewsbury through Upton Magna en route to London after taking over from 7818 and 2200, 24 September 1960. This would have been an Old Oak Castle turn during the week. The later headboard has been transferred from 7818 to 5059. (T.E. Williams)

Old Oak's double-chimney King, 6015 *King Richard III,* approaches Shrewsbury with the down *Cambrian Coast Express* on the same day, 24 September 1960. It has seven chocolate & cream Mark 1 coaches and three strengthening vehicles including a Gresley LNER teak coach at the rear. Old Oak has used an older style headboard on this occasion. (T.E. Williams)

7818 *Granville Manor* returns to Machynlleth and Aberystwyth single-handed, accelerating away from Shrewsbury, the ex-LNER coach now at the front, 24 September 1960. 7818 was Machynlleth's choice for the *Cambrian Coast Express* that summer, David Maidment's run a few weeks earlier having the same locomotive from Welshpool as at high peak the heavy train avoided Shrewsbury station, the London King having been replaced for the Wolverhampton-Welshpool section by a pair of West Midland allocated engines. (T.E. Williams)

7803 *Barcote Manor* arriving at Dovey Junction with the Aberystwyth portion of the down *Cambrian Coast Express*, 24 August 1961. It is formed of Mark 1 chocolate & cream coaches, has the later headboard and 7803 sports a Collett 'intermediate' tender – unusual for a Manor. (MLS/R.W. Miller collection)

7823 *Hook Norton Manor* leaving Machynlleth with the Aberystwyth portion of the *Cambrian Coast Express*, c1962. (Andrew Dyke collection)

'Pride in the job' – three engine cleaners and the crew of 7802 *Bradley Manor* pose with the engine they have prepared for the up *Cambrian Coast Express* at Aberystwyth shed, c1963. 7800 *Torquay Manor* is also booked off shed with a following stopping train. (Andrew Dyke colourisation/Rail on Line)

7819 *Hinton Manor*, now preserved, heads the up *Cambrian Coast Express*, 8.20am from Pwllheli, at Welshpool, 29 August 1963. Note the strengthening Gresley coach once more in the formation. (MLS)

7812 *Erlestoke Manor*, now preserved, enters Machynlleth station with the down *Cambrian Coast Express*, 3 July 1964. The chocolate & cream set has been replaced by standard maroon Mark 1 vehicles and the headboard is no longer carried. (MLS)

Collett 0-6-0 2236 approaching Towyn with the Pwllheli portion of the *Cambrian Coast Express*, 30 June 1964. By this time the train was formed of BR maroon Mark 1 rather than chocolate & cream carriages and the loco north of Machynlleth bore no headboard. The Collett 0-6-0 has been painted BR passenger lined green, but the locomotive shows signs of neglect and has lost its front numberplate. The train has even lost its express passenger headcode and is now indicated as a stopping service. (MLS)

Two filthy Standard '4' 4-6-0s climb Talerddig bank on the last steam hauled up *Cambrian Coast Express*, formed of maroon Mark 1 stock and without any locomotive headboard, 2 September 1966. (MLS)

MEMORIES OF WORKING ON THE CAMBRIAN

In this chapter we gain a glimpse of life working on the railway, keeping the wheels turning. Paul Carpenter contacted and interviewed a number of men who worked on the Cambrian section and met them to hear their stories.

We start with Brian Rowe, who Paul first met in the early 1990s on a visit to Oswestry. He was chairman of the Cambrian Railways Society at the time and passionate to recreate the railway in the town. His drive and commitment to that vision was inspiring. It is a major factor for this book, to ensure that his efforts, and those of the current volunteers, are not forgotten. Brian lost his fight against cancer in 2017.

Oswestry Loco Works Staff - 1955

This photo shows the men from the works who kept the locomotive fleet operational – such as BR 2MT 2-6-0 78006 here, c1955. John Dyke found the photo and John Morris managed to name everyone involved. (John Dyke/John Morris)

Wilfred Allison, Thomas Marshall, Walter Ancell, Cyril Williams, Tony Watkins, Stan Taylor, Donald Bound, Alan Seddon, Alan Parks, John Morris, Taff Evan, Mike Jones, Billy Gillespey

Tony Pritchard, Arthur Kynaston, Albert Jones, Ernie Hinder, Dai Wynne, Leo Jones, Bill Evan, Ormsby Williams, Don Rees, Tom Evan, Jack Evans or Edwards

Nutty Price, Dai Vaughan, Freddy Phillips, Herbert Jones, Albert Jones, Ted Jones, Jack Edward (Foreman), Ernest Hampson, Bert Cawley, Horace Payne, Jack Whitby, Dai Vaughan, Arthur Lindup, Gerald Tanner

Brian Rowe, Oswestry Fireman, 1952-1964

On a hot Summer morning in 2016, Brian Rowe recalled his early days working for British Railways at Oswestry:

In the summer of 1952 I completed my studies at Oswestry Technical College on a Friday and started work for British Railways the following Monday. I was seventeen years old and employed as a booking boy in Oswestry North Signal Box. Over the next nine months I learned all the bell codes but discovered that I wasn't greatly interested in signals or being stuck indoors in a box. One day my old school chum Norman Roberts came up to the box requesting a route to go light engine to Moat Lane Junction. It happened to be a lovely sunny day and I was so envious that he was riding around the country on an engine whilst I was stuck in the box.

I told the signalman that I really fancied getting out on the engines and wanted to apply for a transfer. He did all he could to talk me out of it saying that I was already in the best place. Finally, he reluctantly sent me to see the Oswestry Station Master who also tried to talk me out of a transfer. Once he realised that I was determined to join the Locomotive Department he arranged an interview for me at Swindon. I well recall that day; I was given a thorough medical which included very demanding eye tests. Having passed these, I left there with a brown paper bag containing the magical "grease top" cap and overalls. As I stood on Swindon station waiting for a train home, a "King" rushed through the station going "like the clappers". I was so excited to think that, one day, I could be on that engine. The thrill and feeling of excitement of that day has always remained with me.

I returned to Oswestry and started work as a cleaner. Typically, the loco fleet comprised Manors, Panniers and 14XXs with a few 'Dukedogs' and Prairies. After some ten months I was waiting for vacancies to become a Passed Cleaner. Effectively this was a case of dead man's shoes so I applied for a transfer to Old Oak Common to obtain promotion and got it. I stayed at Old Oak Common for nine months after which I applied for a transfer back to Oswestry and returned as a Passed Cleaner.

At Oswestry my first job as fireman was in No.1 Oswestry Shunt and naturally this involved a lot of shunting. There were three "Shunt Rosters" – "Oswestry Shunt", "Works Shunt" and "Branch Shunt". We had several 16XX Pannier tanks and these were the usual motive power for these duties. A typical day required signing on shed at 7am with a finishing time of 6.30 pm. Days were long and physical but there was also a lot of waiting around – those 16XX were great little engines and very comfortable for a quick nap!

The "Works Shunt" involved taking a pannier into the works at 8am to remove all the wagons repaired the previous day and replacing them with another load. We would go in again at lunchtime to remove any other wagons. I always felt bad about this trip as the fitters were all sitting around having their lunch and we would fill the whole place with smoke! The wagons would all come out gleaming in "Battleship Grey" and this repair work went on endlessly dealing with thousands of wagons.

'As my route knowledge increased, I was assigned regular trips on the Llanfyllin goods, Tanat goods and Newtown goods. These were wonderful for developing skills and confidence and I just loved working up the lines and being out on the locos. The morning goods to Llanfyllin was a truly idyllic journey through beautiful countryside and just a few stops. Several cottages were along the line and often the occupants would leave bottles perched on their gate posts for target practice. The crew would throw lumps of coal at these and the residents collected up free fuel! The engine for this branch was usually a 46XX although a 16XX often appeared

My regular driver at this time was "Black Jack" – a nickname well earned because he never washed. One day Jack sent me up to Llynclys signal box to collect the token and added "the signalmen will have something for you". To my amazement it was a 410 gun. Jack would shoot rabbits and pheasants as we trundled along and sold them to the local pub at Llanfyllin. In the days when a loco was shedded at this

branch line terminus, Jack used to sleep overnight in the shed. We delivered a lot of coal to Llanfyllin. Many children went to school in this town and the trains were always full of kids before 9am and after 4pm. We had a regular guard, Tom Lunt, and he ruled those kids with a rod of iron. Any nonsense was quickly dealt with by him and often involved a "clip round the ear." We also spent a lot of time moving stone trains around the system and the last trip of the day usually involved bringing a stone train back to Oswestry.

When I was in the "Top Goods Link" I usually had the same driver. The driver is the governor on the footplate and how they conduct themselves and treat their fireman tended to vary greatly. If the driver wasn't talkative – and many weren't – it could be a long and lonely day. In this link I not only had a driver who never spoke, he would regularly fall asleep in his seat. He smoked constantly so all the time I could see a glow at the end of his cigarette I knew he was awake. His routine never changed; he would set the reverser to 35%, puff on his cigarette and nod off. One night he was sound asleep in his seat and I decided that enough was enough. I took the coal pick, walked up behind him and hit the side of the cab with it as hard as I could. He jumped up completely startled and started shouted and swearing. I said to him" Don't you ever fall asleep on this engine again" – and he didn't! Other than the diagram "Gobowen Stone to Oxley Sidings", we never saw a signal.

Oswestry Shed had three links – Bottom Goods, Top Goods and Bottom Passenger. The "Bottom Passenger" link had some lovely rosters. Locally we would run to Llanfyllin, Ellesmere, Wrexham and Gobowen. The Wrexham and Gobowen trips usually used a 14XX running in "push-pull" operation. We used to love the run to Gobowen as we could chat up all the girls going to work at the orthopaedic hospital. We nicknamed the train "The Inter-Titty" and our chat up lines must have impressed as I wound up marrying two of them!

Longer runs would take us to Aberystwyth and I regularly fired on two of these. The first left Oswestry at 8.20 am with a first stop at Llanymynech. We then only stopped at Welshpool, Newtown, Machynlleth, Dovey Junction before arriving at Aberystwyth. This was an easy trip for the fireman as the fire needed little attention once it was made up. A second train left Oswestry at 10.50 for Aberystwyth and this was a different story. It stopped everywhere and this "knocked hell" out of the fire. You were forever on the shovel. Compared to other diagrams the Aberystwyth trips were good but long hard days.

Another "interesting" journey was the late Saturday night train through Moat Lane Junction. This was a station in the middle of nowhere with the only access by footpath. This encouraged late night drinking as the local "bobby" couldn't get to this area quickly. Every Saturday night, without fail, the last trains used to take those 'lads' home, drunk and singing their heads off. The poor guard always had a tough time as these characters were difficult to get on the train and even harder to get off! Moat Lane also had a large marshalling yard and had its own engine shed for those trains.

In those days everyone had a nickname and it seemed like everyone was a character. There was "Jimmy the Jip", Chunky Williams, Porky Milner, Calendar Jack, Black Jack, Seldom Rowe and Tip Dyke to name just a few. Seldom was my elder brother Tony and his nickname stemmed from "seldom seen working"! Calendar Jack earned his name due to his craving for overtime. It was said that Jack never looked at his watch, only his calendar. I was known as "Rowie", for obvious reasons.

During my time on shed at Oswestry there were 52 sets of crews with a fleet of 48 engines. These ranged from Panniers, a Prairie, 'Dukedog' Manors, Class 2 Tender engines and some Class 3 Tanks. Around this time the Manors were gradually being replaced by the BR Standard 75XXX engines. These were much more

comfortable for the crews, especially at remote locations like Dovey Junction with a Force 8/9 gale blowing at 45 degrees to the train, but they just did not steam like a Manor. The Oswestry Shed was always very busy with most of the engines usefully employed nearly all the time. This was a lively place to work and I loved it.

On one occasion driver Harry Evans and I were rostered to take a freight train to Oxley sidings and the motive power was usually a Manor. This day we were surprised and concerned to see we had been allocated a 'Dukedog'. I complained to Shedmaster Fred Rolands but he said, "Less of your cheek lad and just get on with the job." The engine steamed beautifully, and we had a delightful ride. At Oxley sidings another driver, from Birmingham, came over and asked, "Where's the 'Coy'?" I didn't understand his accent or question so asked him to repeat it. Again, he enquired about the "Coy" but then, looking at the engine, asked, "It is clockwork isn't it ?!" My driver was furious.

Every trip was always different for many reasons, but a few particular incidents come to mind. Talerdigg always presented a formidable challenge to the crews. Towards the summit at Bells Bridge there are reverse curves on a 1 in 52 gradient, so you needed to have your wits about you. I recall a couple of occasions when we were working the "Double Home Goods" to Aberystwyth. We would arrive there at 7.30am. We should have stayed in lodgings in the town, but we usually slept in the Guards Van and spent the allowance down the pub! Later that day the routine was to back onto our train in Aberystwyth at 5.30pm for a 6.30 departure for arrival back at Oswestry at 11pm. We generally followed the mail train all the way back to Oswestry. Black Jack was my driver and when all was well he would sing – he loved to sing. On this particular trip we were running short of steam half way up to Talerdigg so I asked Jack to stop for five minutes for a "blow up". He refused. It was clear to me that we were never going to make it over the top, so I walked across the footplate and put the brakes on. Jack was not amused but I needed to clean the fire, top up the boiler and bring the pressure up to the mark. Under the glare from my driver I sorted the fire out and gave the "right away" as quickly as I could. Part of the job of the fireman is to check the train before departure and get a wave from the guard. In my haste, on this occasion, I didn't.

Further along the line, where the road runs parallel to the track, Jack was busily singing again when he suddenly screamed out "You bloody fool Rowie". Looking across to the road Jack saw our guard on the back of a motorbike waving his fist at us. He must have got down from the train and we had left without him! We stopped at the next station and waited for him but when he caught us up he never said a word to me then or later – ever! Jack also had the last laugh as for years afterwards he would have a gentle dig and enquire, "Sure the Guard's there Rowie?"

We did stop on Talerdigg on another occasion when the engine was steaming freely but it couldn't cope with the load of wagons we were taking back to Oswestry. Again, it was clear that we would not make it to the top, so we stopped and decided that we would have to split the train. It was in November and getting dark, so we left the guard with the rear portion of the train protected by detonators, whilst we struggled on to the next signal box to explain what was happening. The signalman was not best pleased as by this time he was holding an express from the section. We shunted the first section of the train into a siding and then ran back, wrong road for the second portion. Eventually out of the blackness the tail lamps came into view and the detonators went off as we inched our way back. We hooked on and, checking that the guard was on board, got underway. When we eventually got back to Oswestry, still puzzled why this trip had been so difficult, we discovered that all the wagons were crippled and condemned and were being returned for scrapping. Their bearings had probably not seen oil for months if not years!

The winter of 1963 was a particularly harsh one with extensive snow and sub- zero temperatures. Another of my friends, "Tip" Dyke, was rostered to take the 21.28 mail train from Oswestry to Whitchurch where they would shunt the stock into the bay and turn on the turntable before running light engine to Salop. The temperature was minus eight degrees Celsius and the vacuum operated turntable at the shed had frozen and could not be used. This made it necessary for the crew to run to Salop tender first. Western engines are well known for their poor weather protection of the crew and running tender first in such temperatures must have been truly freezing and a dreadful experience. At Salop they then worked the "Penzance Parcels" to Crewe before working back through Whitchurch to Oswestry, arriving at 4am. The fireman was twenty-year-old Norman Roberts, but driver Dyke was in his sixties and less able to cope with the extreme cold. On arrival at Oswestry he was so cold he could not get off the engine himself and had to be virtually carried down. Shortly afterwards he suffered a massive stroke which left him unable to move or speak before his eventual demise.

Whilst at Oswestry I was called up to serve two years National Service. I spent nineteen months in Kenya and, on return, found it very difficult to re-adjust back into society. Towards the end Oswestry Shed became a sad place to work. The branches were closing, and morale was very low. We used to sign on at 10am for a job entitled "As required". In practice we played cards all day long, lost money and got very depressed. All that we had served with such passion for so long was falling apart around us – and there was nothing we could do. Some drivers transferred to other sheds still operating and would move to Wrexham, Crewe, Salop and Stafford Rd. Inevitably closure followed shed closure.

I could see the ways things were going, decided that this "gypsy life" was not for me and left in 1964. Oswestry Shed closed in 1965 and the last train to Gobowen ran in 1966 when the line and all the branches were closed completely. People don't often realise the impact that the closure of the railway had on the local towns. Most people still used the railway to travel to work or go shopping and it often meant people moving to be able to get to work. The whole town of Oswestry appeared to be in shock – a blow from which it has never fully recovered. I too moved away to work in engineering in Telford. To make matters worse the two other major employers in the area, Park Hall Camp and the local colliery, also closed at this time. Collectively the impact was devastating. Some men had spent 40 years working on the railway and were quite lost without this way of life.'

Colin Vaughan – Oswestry Fireman 1952-1964

Colin worked as a fireman at Oswestry shed but currently lives in Australia. Through many emails and letters, he fondly recalls his experiences from those days and the characters he worked with:

I was born in Oswestry and grew up with a large group of local lads. At fifteen years of age in 1952, I left school and applied for a job on the railway in Oswestry. In honesty, there was not much choice of work in those days, it was either the farm, the pits or the railway. My first interview was in the Works office and included a medical followed by a second interview at Swindon, which I passed.

I always wanted to work on the footplate but, at that time, there were no vacancies for cleaners. I was sent into the main Works and spent three months as a rivet boy and assigned to Jack. Jack was a heavy smoker and was always asking me to light his "roll up" cigarettes. This sounds simple enough, but the cigarette was always hanging out of his mouth and he expected me to light it using the end of the red-hot rivet straight out of the forge – my hands would always shake for fear of burning his nose!

Eventually a vacancy for a cleaner came up and I got the job. On the first day I was assigned to fireman Harry Watson and he showed me what I had to do. The charge-hand was Syd Roberts and he was not keen on the cleaners being helped with their work, although he turned a "blind eye" to it. We, in turn, would help the firemen prepare their engines. The work was hard and dirty, but there was a great spirit among the lads, we were young and just got on with it.

My first turn as a "Passed Cleaner" was on the No. 2 Pilot. The driver was Gerald Martin and it was also his first day as a driver – we made a very cautious pair setting about our tasks. I continued cleaning engines well into 1953 when I had turned sixteen years old. Then something unexpected happened. Forty Firemen vacancies were advertised at Tyseley Shed and, together with my mates Gaga Paine and Dennis Lloyd, we all applied and were offered posts. It turned out that the local "Bird's Custard" factory in Tyseley were advertising for lots of staff and the money and working conditions offered were far better than those as railway firemen. Perhaps many were anticipating the end of steam on the railways. Money was tight, so ten of us shared one room in a local boarding house in Tyseley which was run by an elderly couple. Every meal included cheese in various disguises and, although we dropped many hints, including letting wind-up mice loose, the landlady never got the message. I had been at Tyseley for twelve months when a firing vacancy became available back at Oswestry. I applied for the job and returned to my "home" shed.

The work at Oswestry was varied and occasionally took me into the main Works if I was assigned to the "Works Shunt" roster. This also occasionally involved delivering or collecting an engine from the "top end" locomotive repair section of the works. One of the hardest days I had at Oswestry was on engine 6342. We had worked the mail train from Oswestry to Machynlleth and changed platforms to bring 6342 back to Oswestry with the returning mail train. As the crew handed over the engine, they said that it would be a miracle if we made it back up Talerdigg.

When I inspected the fire, I discovered that all the tubes were leaking, and the front of the fire was out – we made it but only just!

We worked on a variety of classes of locomotives at Oswestry, but the Manors were always my favourite. They were ideal for the work and always made plenty of steam. That said, the operating conditions became a lot better with the arrival of the "Standards". Oswestry were allocated Standard Class 2 tender engines, Standard Class 3 tanks and Standard Class 4 tender and tank engines. Crew protection from the elements was far superior to the Western cab layouts, as were the positioning of the controls. I also worked on some old Cambrian engines for a while and I fired on the last two "Dean Goods" engines allocated to Oswestry, 2538 and 2516. The latter is now preserved at the "STEAM" museum on the site of the old Works at Swindon.

Oswestry Shed operated a two-shift system with twelve crews on each shift. Some of the names of crew were Gaga Paine, Dennis Lloyd, Hilliam, Norman and Keith Roberts – all brothers and Tony, Brian and Mike Rowe – also brothers. We all worked long hours and the work was heavy, dirty and often hard, but the camaraderie of the men was great – we always found things to laugh about and they were always good to work with. I never seemed to have much to do with the shed foreman – we simply got on with the jobs we were given. There were also approximately twelve fitters permanently on duty in the shed, attending to a wide range of engine reported faults from leaking valves and clacks to a full motion strip down. Heavier work, like axlebox refurbishment, required a visit to Oswestry works.

I carried on working trains at Oswestry for some 12 months before being called up for National Service on 8 May 1956. Tony Rowe was also called up on the same day and we both spent the next two years in Kenya. Upon return, in 1958, we simply carried on with our firing duties. I remained firing at Oswestry until 1964 when I decided it was time to leave. Everything was getting very run down and morale of the men was low. It just wasn't the enjoyable job it used to be, and it was clear that the end was not far away.'

John Morris – Steam Locomotive Fitter Oswestry Works 1952-1963

John Morris is a railway enthusiast and comes from a family of proud railwayman. His great grandfather was employed by the GWR at Gobowen and his father also worked for British Railways at Oswestry. The railway environment is a tough and potentially dangerous place to work – John's Uncle Jim was killed on the line and John's father also died at work, aged only 46 years old.

To this day, John proudly shows the tools and booklets he was issued on his first day – tools which date back to Cambrian times. Some of his workmates had started their careers in Cambrian Railways days and the Works provided plenty of knowledge and experience for a keen and budding railwayman.

He started railway life on 12 August 1952, aged just fourteen. A railway friend of the family arranged an interview and, following some basic tests including colour blindness, John became an apprentice fitter in Oswestry Locomotive Works, embarking upon a four-year apprenticeship. Generally, this followed a format and programme that assigned an apprentice with a qualified fitter in each section of the fitting department. Here he would first be shown and then expected to deliver all the various tasks within that section. Normally this continued for three months before being moved to the next section with another fitter. Learning on the job was very much the approach taken and, although some considered this cheap labour, it ensured that the apprentice became a productive member of the engineering gang. Oswestry Works never built new engines, but it was rated as one of the more important maintenance centres within the GWR system. Collett himself visited the works to emphasise its importance.

John's first year on the railway was not actually spent in the Works but largely in Oswestry running shed. Here, duty fitters were always on standby and they carried out minor maintenance repairs on engines in service. These would typically include repacking glands and stuffing boxes, changing sight feed glasses, and generally addressing any problems reported by the driver. By the end of the year John had been shown and was experienced and competent to repair all the above as well as leaking clacks, safety valves, regulators and any other minor maintenance tasks. The second year saw John assigned to the 'Outdoor Gang' and here he found himself working up and down the line as far afield as Welshpool and Newtown. The work involved the repair of outdoor plant and equipment and typically included maintaining pumps, cranes, compressors, gantries, etc. By the end of this year, he had acquired a very broad knowledge of most of the mechanical equipment found on a railway – and he was still only sixteen years old.

Year three found John back in the works but now being trusted to carry out work with little supervision. It was now that he became increasingly aware of a variety of working practices and constraints that affected both his learning and pay packet. The 'War Bonus' was stopped and everyone was now paid on a flat rate but with a shift allowance. The Works was manned on a two-shift system of 6am to 3pm and 3pm to 11pm and this created difficulties for the charge hands who were often short of men to 'pinch bar' cold engines into the Works. John also discovered that skilled men were often unwilling to pass on their knowledge to apprentices or assist fellow workers who might be from a different section of the works. On one occasion, he helped a boiler fitter who was struggling to crawl out of the firebox through the firehole door with a bag of tools. Had he been spotted doing this he would have been in trouble. Men trained in 'white metalling' and valve setting, for example, tended to act as a secret society and would never show anyone their 'art'. Job protection was paramount, and knowledge perceived as their only bargaining tool.

During this year, John spent a lot of time turning up bearings for big ends and coupling rods, brake rigging, etc. He also was allocated to the 'Coal Tender' section which again was mainly turning jobs for water valves, scopes, linkages, etc. He recalls that any work inside the tank was very unpleasant due to the restricted, dark space and the stench of dead fish!

The fourth year continued to require working on similar tasks, but he was now deemed competent to have an apprentice working with him – he was now providing the instruction. Typically, John would be tackling jobs like setting up slide bar using inside micrometers to ensure they were parallel. This could be a very tricky job and often very time consuming. He recalls that, in general, the works were becoming quite quiet and there was a feeling that everything was being run down. The apprentice programme required that part of this year was spent working away at Stafford Road Works. Here, there was much more activity and work, so this part of the training was varied and interesting.

John's apprenticeship ended in April 1956, but he was only back in Oswestry a month before he commenced National Service. On his return to Oswestry, he returned to the fitting gang and was working in the smokebox of an engine, removing the blastpipe, when he was sent for by the Works Manager Mr. Goodman. The manager made it quite clear that the works were being run down but that he was obliged to retain anyone returning from National Service for a period of six months. However, he was free to leave earlier if a suitable job arose. John returned to the shop floor and was again inside the filthy smokebox when a messenger appeared requesting that he return to Mr. Goodman's office and clean off the black marks his boots had made on his carpet! Knowing he was under notice, John refused, and nothing more came of the incident.

In October 1956, John was working with a fitter gang when an engine that had just returned from repair at Stafford Road was found to be leaking badly. The Oswestry fitters refused to work on it and insisted that it be returned to Stafford Road to be repaired properly. A charge hand and fitter were dispatched from Stafford Road to Oswestry to inspect the problem and recognised John from his previous time working with them. They immediately offered him a permanent job back at Stafford Road and he started the next day! John had been earning £ 7 7s 11d a week on returning to Oswestry and he was now offered £14 a week with overtime at Stafford Road where he worked for three years until the Works closed. John completed his career with ICI but his training and experiences at Oswestry had made him a much sought-after craftsman.

John Dyke – Apprentice Boilersmith Oswestry Works, 1958-1963

When John left school his ambition was to be a motor mechanic. Unfortunately, such work was in short supply and he was unable to obtain an apprenticeship in this trade. To improve his chances of employment, he attended evening classes and studied a City and Guilds Craft course, but still no suitable apprenticeship was available.

Through a friend and family connection, an interview was arranged at the Locomotive Carriage and Wagon Works in Oswestry and John was offered a five-year scheme as an apprentice boilersmith. As there were no vacancies for locomotive fitters, which would probably have suited him better, he embarked upon this apprenticeship and entered Oswestry Works in January 1958 aged just under sixteen. The attraction to this course was the training offered in welding.

John's first impression of the works was that it resembled something from the Victorian era. All machines were belt driven from overhead shafts seemingly running everywhere. The only machine driven by an electric motor was the wheel lathe. The works were dirty and very noisy. He rather wondered what he had let himself in for. It was evident that the works had had no investment for many years with only essential maintenance tasks being carried out.

On his first day, John was introduced to Arthur Kynaston, who was the acting boilersmith chargeman. Arthur assigned John to work with a boilersmith. It was clear that there was little boiler repair going on and that the repair of steam locomotive boilers was being phased out. In fact, there did not seem to be very much work going on throughout the whole Works.

His first job was to change the fusible plug inside a locomotive's firebox. This involved crawling into the box, unscrewing the old plug, re-tapping the threads and sealing a new plug in place. He was then shown how to 'caulk' stays and seams and these occurred mainly in the fire area of the firebox. Tasks like removing and replacing stays were all undertaken from inside the firebox and John was to spend much of his time in this cramped, noisy and sometimes still hot environment. Shortly after John started the locomotive works changed its title to the 'Heavy Maintenance Repair Depot' and this more accurately described the typical work undertaken there.

The apprenticeship course did not appear to follow any structured format but rather to respond to the workload of jobs as they appeared in the section. There was no exam or assessment at the end of each year to ensure competence and progression was taken for granted. However, over the duration of the course, every process for the maintenance of boilers was experienced and learned. Safety in the works was always taken seriously but not all hazards were known and identified as such at the time. John recalls that many of the gaskets used on boilers, for example on the steam inner dome, involved working with white asbestos and it was only in later years the real danger of this material to health was realised. Boiler shops were also known to be one of the noisiest sections within the works and it was common for boilersmiths to suffer loss of hearing; John too suffered 'Noise Induced Hearing Loss' which was only identified and recognised and acknowledged much later.

During the first year of the course, all tasks were strictly under the supervision of a boilersmith. Again, the old issue of job protection was in evidence with boilersmiths only passing on the minimum information. John was particularly keen to develop his welding skills as he had a natural aptitude for this work and realised that this skill would be transferable to any industry in the future and would certainly outlast work on steam boilers. The shop welders were again reluctant to show him more than the minimum. Fortunately, the apprenticeship course provided one day a week attendance at a college and here he met A.C. Davis, a college lecturer who was passionate and expert about welding and had written the standard book on the subject. Under Mr. Davis, John quickly became very competent and this was a real asset to him throughout his career.

John's tasks in the boiler section gradually became less about repairing boilers by traditional methods and more about welding repairs to carry the pressure vessel through its few remaining years. During his five-year course, which was largely repetitive types of welding repairs, the boilersmith apprenticeship was shortened to three years. He always thought that the apprenticeship was too long and largely served as a source of cheap labour. The change led to younger apprentices on the new course becoming qualified and earning more ahead of those completing their five-year course.

At the end of his apprenticeship, John stayed at the Works for a further year. Repairs on boilers continued to decline and he applied for a Technical Assistant's post at Chester, which he was offered. He was now involved with the maintenance of cranes, plant and machinery as well as continuing with his studies at college. Interestingly, one of his jobs was to return to the old Works where part of it was now rented out to a private company. His task was to calculate what proportion of the Works heating bill should be attributable to the private company.

His technical knowledge and experience had now broadened in this new role and this eventually led to a job outside the railway working for Metro Cammell, which later became Alstom. John speaks very respectfully of the quality of work and standards delivered by the German engineers. Once again, the sound training that was given in Oswestry Works had formed the foundation of a later career in the outside world.

Sidney Lloyd – Fireman at Machynlleth, 1938-1988

Sidney Lloyd was born into a family of railwaymen and so, on leaving school, it was inevitable that he would work on the railway. His father was a 'Ganger' – a foreman with half a dozen men under him. He was responsible for the tracks on the Brecon-Newport line, including the fierce seven-mile gradient between Talybont and Torpantau, which he remembers as being his father's biggest worry.

Following an introduction by his dad and an interview at Swindon, Sidney started at Machynlleth Shed as an engine cleaner. He was fourteen years of age. At that time, unemployment was very high, so a railway career offered a secure job with opportunities for promotion.

On his first day, Sid reported to the shed foreman who showed him around and explained what was expected of him. He was introduced to Bill Jones, who had been an engine cleaner at the shed for ten years. This length of time reflected how few opportunities and vacancies there were at that time, due to the economic slump. Sid recalls that the shed was full of engines, typically including Prairie tanks and tender locos of the Dean Goods classes together with the more modern 22XXs.

Sid only worked as a cleaner for twelve months due to the outbreak of war. Suddenly men were in short supply, promotions had to be accelerated and Sid became a 'Passed Cleaner.' He thinks that this promotion was probably too fast as the traditional promotion structure was a safe system, allowing time to become familiar with all the engine parts. The lowest link at a shed was usually shunting in the yard and this allowed plenty of time to discuss the art of firing and 'enginemanship' with the driver. Learning 'on the job' was considered the best way. At Machynlleth, the links were Yard, Slow Goods, Fast Goods, Local Passenger and Fast Passenger. Once out of the yard, Sid fired freight trains to Oswestry, Shrewsbury and Wolverhampton, picking up wagons from the good yards along the Cambrian main line. At that time the Cambrian line carried a high volume of freight traffic and shunting yards were full of wagons to be transported far and wide.

Sid always enjoyed his trips around the region except if the allocated engine would not steam. There were several members of the 22XX class that were dreaded for this reason, making life even more challenging on the footplate. Tank engines were always limited on water capacity and stopping to 'put the bag in' was a regular occurrence especially with the steep inclines like Talerddig. When the Manors were allocated to Machynlleth, no-one was happier than Sid. He recalls that they were always free steaming and made the job much easier and enjoyable. They quickly became his favourite engines. He refers to them as 'The Torpedos' due to the taper barrel on their boilers.

Sid gradually worked his way up through the links and was involved in staff and management issues. He became the representative for the Local Departmental Committee (LDC). This involved presenting footplate crew issues and grievances to the regional management. He attended regular meetings with Mr. Snell who was the Line Superintendent based in Oswestry. He recalls that Snell controlled everything but was a very pleasant man and an excellent engineer.

In 1956, having completed some 250 driving turns as a 'Passed Fireman', Sid was promoted to driver and transferred to Tyseley. From here, he regularly drove ten coach passenger trains into Paddington and looks back with some anguish at how they had to stop such heavy loads so close to the buffers; that responsibility seems to startle him now. He speaks very fondly of the Castle class engines which he says handled such trains with ease. When the Standard class locomotives were introduced Sid was delighted. The Great Western locos were never designed for crew comfort and Sid appreciated being able to drive from a sitting position.

As steam was phased out, Sid was sent to Derby for retraining on diesels which he drove until his retirement in 1988. He witnessed all the consequences of the Beeching cuts and is firmly of the view that they went too far and were a mistake. He also witnessed the congestion on the roads which could not cope with the increasing amount of traffic. Sid is currently 95 and loves to recall the 'good old days' when he worked on the railway.

Dave Owen – Modern Day Steam Locomotive Engineer, 1975-2016

We have seen from earlier stories the types of work carried out in Oswestry Works to service and maintain steam locomotives. With all the purpose-built tools and equipment available in the Works, the overhaul of steam engines still required a great deal of physical strength and ingenuity. Imagine then how much harder it would be to undertake such work without any special tools and equipment or even a building to protect from the weather. This has been the starting point for many heritage railways and was certainly the case in the early days of the Llangollen Railway.

Dave Owen is the son of Ivor Owen who started as a cleaner at Shrewsbury Shed in 1944, became a fireman at Croes Newydd in 1949 and driver in 1961. Dave's grandfather, Frank Owen, had previously started at Salop in 1919, becoming a fireman and driver there before transferring to Croes Newydd in 1942.

As a young boy and teenager, Dave grew up around engines and loved visiting the sheds with his dad. Following a successful career at Brymbo Steelworks, Dave visited Oswestry to inspect *Foxcote Manor* which had just been rescued from Barry Scrapyard. The Cambrian Society had only recently formed and there was little in the way of tools, plant and machinery. Dave was invited to visit the Llangollen Railway by his friend and first CME, Bob Maxwell. This railway was also in its infancy but had more volunteers and generally impressed him. Dave started at Llangollen as a volunteer in September 1975. There was no yard or workshop at Llangollen and early repair work was undertaken in the lower room of the signal box which was fitted with only a bench and vice. The Foxcote Manor Society decided that the Llangollen Railway would be better placed to restore their engine. Once again, Dave found himself working on this engine. In 1990, he became a full-time employee of the Llangollen Railway and their Chief Mechanical Engineer after Bob emigrated to Australia. An extension was built to the old goods shed and this became the building in which the Manor was completed. Given the general lack of facilities and, recalling that previously such work was only possible in a locomotive works, this achievement is quite remarkable. In 1991, amid much excitement, *Foxcote Manor* hauled its first passenger train in preservation and went on to become the flagship locomotive of the railway for the next thirty odd years.

Dave oversaw the construction of a new four road shed in 1994 and this allowed further restoration work to be undertaken. With the new shed being used for maintenance, it became possible to convert the old goods shed to a machine shop. As more facilities and machinery became available, and with the employment of a full-time machinist, it became possible to stop contracting parts out for machining and undertake all machining work in-house. In 2002, an apprenticeship scheme was set up and this has developed many trainees into fully competent steam engineers that are much in demand with other railways.

In 2016, Dave retired as CME of the railway. His friendly manner and passion for high standards of workmanship have been greatly missed. He continues to offer his knowledge and expertise to railway projects and is the Resident Engineer for the Night Owl project. His achievements in preserving and developing the skills to repair and maintain steam locomotives is a major component in the success of the Llangollen Railway and follows closely in the footsteps of all those dedicated engineers from Oswestry and other Works who thoroughly understood the steam engine and gave their all to keep them in working order.

Dave Owen at Llangollen with the 'Manor' he restored, 7822 *Foxcote Manor*. (Paul Carpenter)

FROM BRITISH RAILWAYS TO TRANSPORT FOR WALES (TfW)

The Impact of the Beeching cuts in the 1960s

Following the First World War, public use of the rail national network was in decline. There were many social and economic reasons for this, but the trend continued into the 1960s and led to British Railways incurring huge annual losses. Uneconomic branch lines had already begun to close since the 1920s – some 1,264 miles were closed between 1923 and 1939. In the early 1960s, the government was forced to address this worsening situation and appointed a private sector industrialist to undertake a review of the issues and propose solutions. Richard Beeching became Chairman of British Railways in 1961 and his infamous Beeching Report – 'The Reshaping of British Railways' – was issued on 27 March 1963. In the decade following Beeching's report, some 4,000 miles of track and 3,000 stations were closed, changing the size and shape of the national rail network for ever. Effectively, one third of the network was closed and some 330,000 wagons were also scrapped.

Why is this relevant to the railways in Wales? Simply, because Wales was a classic example of everything that Beeching identified as wrong with railways, i.e. uneconomic, inefficient, long distances between stations, few passengers and goods. Staffing levels were high and the harsh and mountainous landscape created high maintenance costs on many routes.

The report had a significant impact on all aspects of the Cambrian Railways. The main line to Aberystwyth, originally accessed at Whitchurch, was diverted to commence from Shrewsbury via Buttington Junction. At a stroke, all stations from Buttington Junction to Whitchurch were closed, including the branches linking Ellesmere to Wrexham and Llanymynech to Llanfyllin. Numerous intermediate stations along the route to Aberystwyth were either closed or became unstaffed halts with local branch lines also closed and lifted. The proud railway town of Oswestry, which once boasted two stations, was left without one. Oswestry loco shed was closed with many redundancies and the Carriage, Wagon and Locomotive Works followed shortly after with further redundancies. The impact on the town and local villages was severe and is still evident to this day.

The coastal line to Pwllheli remained largely intact but many local stations became unstaffed halts to reduce operating costs. The Cambrian Railways branches were an easy target for cuts and were closed on the dates below:

Ellesmere to Wrexham	Closed 1965
The Tanat Valley	Closed 1952 for passengers – 1964 for freight
The Llanfyllin Branch	Closed 1965
Welshpool and Llanfair	Closed 1956 – reopened as a preservation railway in 1963

The Corris Railway	Closed 1948 – part reopened to passengers in 2002
The Kerry Branch	Closed 1956
The Dinas Mawddwy Branch	Closed 1952

The exception to branch closures was the Vale of Rheidol Railway which was reprieved following the personal intervention of George Dow, who was a senior manager for British Railways.

Surprisingly, no account seems to have been taken of the impact on the main line passenger and freight numbers following closure of these 'feeder' branches. Both in Wales and England, the main line railway passenger numbers fell as car drivers simply drove to their destinations. Those without cars often had to relocate nearer to their work which reduced the local population and further undermined the local economy. Councils, businesses and even the local constabulary fought hard against closures, identifying hardship for the local community as a major risk. Local buses were introduced to replace the train services, but these were slower than the railways they replaced and were often withdrawn within a short period of time.

The Cambrian of the future

Following the radical surgery of Welsh railways and the years of minimalist operations that followed, a new dawn is finally in sight. The Welsh Government is looking at the wealth and prosperity of the nation and has identified that the railway system has a key role to play in achieving this. It is surprising that Beeching did not foresee a day when use of the railways would be increasing, let alone the 50 per cent actual increase experienced in the last ten years. In his defence, he was brought in to manage a financial crisis and imposed a short-term solution that complied with the political pressures of the day. It is also surprising that no account was taken of the needs of the communities, despite many strong protests from all quarters demanding that the needs of the towns and villages be considered. The Welsh government is now correcting these mistakes.

Transport for Wales (TfW) is a 'not for profit' business set up and wholly owned by the Welsh Government to provide Wales with the transport systems it needs for the country to thrive and prosper. A £5 billion investment programme has been produced, designed to transform the current transport systems to customer focussed services. TfW is a delivery organisation whose purpose is to achieve the objectives of the government's economic action plans, which includes a fully integrated transport system across Wales. This will ensure that communities are properly connected and operational surpluses are reinvested back into transport. This is clearly the right approach and has, at the heart of it, listening to and interfacing with the customers – a complete reversal of the Beeching approach. This is to be applauded.

TfW has awarded a 15-year franchise to an Operator and Development Partner (ODP), Keolis – Amey. Keolis will focus on upgrading the existing routes by providing new trains, refurbishing stations and equipping them with modern ticketing and information systems. Amey will concentrate on a new metro system in South Wales. The unique part of this arrangement lies in its interface with Community Rail Officers (CRO) who are employed by the local authorities but who have an ear in the community and a voice with ODP and TfW. The concept of 'community rail' is not new and has been operating effectively across local areas in both England and Wales. The Association of Community Rail Partnerships (ACoRP) is a body that seeks to promote 'social inclusion, economic development and community involvement'. Currently, there are five Community Rail Officers in Wales, but this will be expanded to twelve as part of the new franchise. When meeting these officers, one cannot but be impressed with their awareness of local community needs and desires. They are very effective in making good ideas become reality and are passionate and committed to creating a railway environment that is a pleasant experience for passengers and local community. There is a vision that the station should be more than a place to catch a train.

A good example of this is Gobowen station, which was a neglected and deteriorating set of classic buildings until CRO Sheila Dee consulted with the community and actioned their wishes. The buildings have now been taken over by a trust and, apart from being restored to their former glory, provide a tea shop and meeting point for locals (run by students from the local college with learning difficulties). There are also offices for a local business and a terminus for the reopening of a rail-link to the hospital. This is in addition to knowledgeable and helpful staff who provide the 'human experience' of buying a train ticket! The station has become the heart of the community and mobilised a spirit of village pride missing for many years. This is community rail working at its best, realising opportunities to make the whole experience pleasant and of community value. On the Cambrian, CRO Claire Williams has listened to local requests to reopen some of the stations that Beeching closed with the result that Bow Street will reopen in 2020 with others to follow.

The current plans of the new franchise for the future development of the Cambrian are as follows:

- Increase in frequency of Aberystwyth <> Shrewsbury weekday services from 0.5 trains per hour (tph)to 1 tph from December 2022
- Increase in frequency of Aberystwyth <> Shrewsbury Sunday services from 0.5 tph to 1 tph from December 2019

- Reduction in Aberystwyth <> Shrewsbury journey time from 108 minutes to 105 minutes from December 2022
- Increase in frequency of Machynlleth <> Pwllheli Sunday services from 3 trains per day to 5 trains per day from December 2019 then to 9 trains per day from May 2023
- Increase in total capacity to and from Birmingham along the Cambrian in the morning peak from December 2022
- Increase in total capacity to and from Birmingham along the Cambrian in the evening peak from December 2019, and a further increase from December 2022
- Introduction of new trains from 2022 increasing capacity from 199 to 202 (2 car) or 316 (3 car) units. Also featuring more bicycle spaces and improved air conditioning.
- Investment and improvement at all TfW operated stations, including:
  - an enhanced cleaning programme by December 2019
  - CCTV systems by March 2020
  - cycle storage facilities by March 2023.
- Additional investment and improvement at Shrewsbury, Borth and Machynlleth stations
- New station at Bow Street (between Borth and Aberystwyth) opens in 2020

These are excellent and much needed service improvements which will further increase passenger numbers in the coming years, perhaps leading to more stations reopening. The new franchise provider is also keen to support the aspirations of local heritage railways and this will be beneficial for all parties.

CAMBRIAN HERITAGE RAILWAYS – THE CAMBRIAN RAILWAYS SECOND COMING

The creation of a heritage line

The majestic Oswestry station lost its passenger services in 1966, when the section from Whitchurch to Buttington Junction was closed as part of the Beeching cuts and Cambrian trains were rerouted to start from Shrewsbury. A single track remained operational through the station for the occasional freight train from Blodwell to Gobowen but this too was withdrawn in 1988.

The Cambrian Railways Society (CRS) was formed in 1972 and comprised local enthusiasts and railwaymen with the objective of returning a steam operated tourist line to this railway town. These volunteers set off with high hopes, big ideas and bundles of enthusiasm but little money. A lease was taken on the goods shed, yard and sidings at Oswestry South; this became the headquarters of the Cambrian Railways Society. They created a museum within the goods shed and issued a quarterly newsletter, recalling stories and photos from the past as well as aspirations for the future. Stock was acquired for operation on the line, most notably the Foxcote Manor Society was set up eventually securing the locomotive and negotiations were entered into with British Rail for use of the line at weekends/bank holidays.

These negotiations were successful, resulting in permission for the CRS to use the line at weekends between Oswestry and Gobowen, but two days prior to the first running day in August 1976, BR withdrew permission! Protests resulted in BR relenting and allowed a diesel hauled service due to the short notice of the cancellation. This service ran on the August Bank holiday in 1976 but was bitter sweet. 1,500 passengers were carried over the two days but after this, BR broke off contact citing 'a breakdown in communications within the British Rail organisation'.

After this setback, the Society decided to remain in Oswestry as a museum and steam centre with regular open and steam days with industrial locomotives in light steam. In 1991, an engine shed, and workshop, was erected to increase the scope of work undertaken on the Society's stock, then a Light Railway Order was obtained in 1995 and the society began to run its first public passenger trains. The return of passenger trains to Oswestry had finally begun in this small but milestone way, although still restricted to the Oswestry south sidings.

In 1996, with the aid of a lottery grant, the society purchased Weston Wharf and this became the fledgling railway's first planned destination and second base. At this time, Brian Rowe was the society chairman and he engaged a contractor to carry out roof repairs at Weston Wharf. The son of the contractor, then only 17 years old, was fascinated by the reconstruction of the railway and became a regular volunteer. Within a short period of time, he had worked across all departments of the project and was passed out to drive steam locos by Brian. Rob Williams was that young man and his commitment and drive for the railway are currently achieving greater progress for the heritage line than at any time previously.

In 1996, Oswestry Council instructed W.S. Atkins to produce a feasibility report to determine the viability of a heritage railway based around Oswestry and the ability of the society to deliver it. The report concluded that a preserved railway was the right attraction for the area but that the Cambrian Railways Society was not capable of delivering and operating it without greater resources and suggested the formation of a Trust to support it.

In 1998, Ken Ryder became involved, bringing a fresh approach to meet the society's long-standing aspirations whilst acting on the Atkins report. He, along with a local Councillor David Lloyd, became heavily involved in setting up a new group, the Cambrian Railways Trust (CRT), and Ken became its first Chairman. This proved a step change in the fortunes of the project. Ken was a dynamic businessman who also owned two 'Manor' class locomotives. He set about rebuilding and strengthening relationships with Oswestry Council and based one of his locomotives, 7821 *Ditcheat Manor*, on the line while it received an overhaul in the Society's workshops. This engine had always been based at Oswestry in BR days, so this was something of a 'homecoming'. Suddenly, there was visible evidence of new life in the project and a general mood of optimism and progress was created. Ken also bought Llynclys station which further added to the feeling of a project going places.

For four years, the CRS and CRT co-existed with the general understanding that the CRT would manage the railway and the CRS would operate it. Although this left some unresolved issues, the two bodies worked side by side for several years and this helped overcome the council's perception that the railway lacked credibility and unity.

During the late 1990s, the sale of the line to the Trust became a real possibility. Ken worked tirelessly to achieve his vision, a sale price for the line was agreed and Oswestry Borough Council were poised to meet the payments – all that was needed was a business plan for restoration and running of the railway. The production of a Trust business plan opened the issue of the Society and Trust relationship. Enthusiasm about the project had got the better of good business sense and the actual details of the arrangement between the Society and Trust had never been worked out. This resulted in a situation where there were now two bodies with almost identical aims and people on each side with differing views. The relationship steadily worsened and reached the point where both sides went their separate ways. The sale offer on the line was withdrawn and Railtrack stated they did not wish to deal with either body and, for the second time, the project seemed all but dead as we entered the new millennium.

With the aid of a European grant, the Trust embarked on rebuilding a section of railway on the dismantled track from Llynclys South to Pen-y-Garreg Lane, Pant. This was brought into passenger use in 2005, using class 101 diesel multiple units and has proved a popular destination for train rides, Santa Specials and Driver Experience Courses. In the meantime, the society established a third base on the Nantmawr branch which was ¾ mile long and had never been lifted. The Society was now working in partnership with a new organisation, the Tanat Valley Light Railway, to achieve the restoration of this line.

Oswestry's magnificent station building, and one-time headquarters of the Cambrian, was now in a state of disrepair. The building was secured by the Borough Council and restored to its former glory.

The ground floor comprised a café, ticket office and display space, but it missed a railway!

In the meantime, Railtrack became Network Rail and they expressed an interest in leasing or disposing of the line once again. The issue of responsibilities and liabilities arose, and Network Rail's preferred option was that Shropshire Council should purchase the line. But the issue about leasing the line to two separate bodies remained and the council wished to see a joint approach. For the railway to move forward and lease the line, it became essential for it to restructure its organisation. By now, Henry Thomas had become chairman of the Trust and Rob Williams chairman of the Society and, although volunteer railways run on a great deal of effort by many, the actions, work and leadership from these two men cannot be underestimated in achieving a re-unification. Following a series of joint meetings, a division of operating responsibilities was agreed in 2007 so that the Society contingent of CRS operated the branch line railway around the old Tanat Valley line from Llynclys to Blodwell expanding out from its Nantmawr branch, whilst the Trust would operate the main line from Oswestry through Weston Wharf. A working arrangement and formal contract were entered into, but the building up of relations between the two groups continued. Joint meetings were held with possible funders, however this revealed that the initial thoughts of two separate projects were likely not to work; nether project could produce sufficient outputs to warrant the capital spend in the initial phases.

It became clear that full re-unification would not only be needed but that there was a will to do it. Cambrian Heritage Railways was born with the founder members being the Trust and Society Chairmen. CHR formally came into being in 2009 with both the Society and Trust handing over management of their assets. It became clear to the Society that the project would naturally centre on Oswestry, so the hard decision was taken to walk away from the Nantmawr Branch and the past years of effort.

The new heritage railway board was expanded to ensure an equal mixture of trustees from the two constituent bodies. Looking at the funding options, a clear project plan was laid out based on the Society and Trust joint meetings. This would see the first phase being Oswestry to Weston and the second phase Weston to Llynclys. The new body was lacking credibility from both being new and the events of recent years. Rob held the view that the only way to change this was to start delivering. Clearly with no funding and limited volunteer effort, this was going to be a hard slog. By now, the railway had been sold to Shropshire Council and CHR had negotiated and agreed leases. Due to some minor land registry issues, the leases could not be signed, but instead agreements to lease were entered into. This would give CHR access to the line immediately and commit both sides to entering into the full lease. The contracts were signed by Rob and Henry on St Patrick's day 2009. After 37 years of trying, the railway was now in the hands of preservationists!

From here on, the work and credibility building has continued. Initially using the society's LRO, passenger services were resumed within the sidings at Oswestry. Whilst these services were running, restoration work continued on the platform and track in front of the station building at Oswestry. In May 2010, the passenger service was extended from the fish dock to Oswestry station proper with the platform being formally opened by the local MP, Owen Paterson. This was the first passenger service since that special day in August 1976, but this time it was possible to use the ticket office and café in what must be the finest station building in preservation.

Since that time Cambrian Heritage Railways has gone from strength to strength and the speed of progress is accelerating. A small grant was made to restore the full platform length at Oswestry and vegetation control was implemented on the whole 8½ miles of line. The full lease was eventually signed in 2014, which then allowed the Transport and Works Order to be transferred to CHR, giving the statutory powers for the line. The running line was extended initially to Middleton Road heading south, and then to Gasworks bridge. At Gobowen, land has been acquired from Network Rail and others so that CHR now owns the line to the stop blocks in the bay platform at Gobowen. CHR has worked in partnership with the Oswestry station building trust, not only to use this building but also in acquiring the station buildings at Gobowen. The frequency and type of services has increased, and steam has now returned to Oswestry as a regular feature after a gap of 12 years. Roger Date is the current CHR Chairman and has played a leading role in all of these developments.

Looking to the short-term future, things are very bright for CHR with the initial phase of Oswestry to Weston well advanced. Gas Works Bridge is receiving a strengthening works by Shropshire Council to permit trains to pass. Oswestry Town Council has also made a £120k grant for capital works to restore the track to Weston. In the very near future Oswestry will have an operational railway once again. CHR is also pursuing the delivery of a full-time public service between Oswestry and Gobowen. This will take the form of a modern sustainable transport unit and is currently at the concept stage. CHR has come a long way since its inception in 2009. In parallel with the above, CHR is forging links with other attractions and interested bodies in the area to explore ways in which they can better work together and support each other. This will provide a more varied and interesting experience for visitors and enthusiasts visiting the area.

A little-known heritage battle – as told by Brian Rowe

'Having travelled the world working in weld inspection I returned to Oswestry in 1988 and became a member of the Cambrian Railways Society. A single road was still in operation through the station as stone was still removed from the quarries by rail until October 1988. The fledging society attempted to purchase the line from Railtrack but they neither had the influence or the money.

'In 1990 I was appointed Chairman of the society and we battled on for several years trying to establish ourselves and gain support. Around this time Tesco decided that the station site would be ideal for a supermarket and they planned to retain the facade of the station building, as the entrance to their store, but demolish the rest. I was quite sickened by this proposal and was desperate to find a way to block it. I met with the Chief Executive of the Borough who said he would see what he could do. We met regularly over a period of months during which time the building was deteriorating – windows were boarded up, the roof was leaking, trees were shooting up and generally the whole thing looked derelict and abandoned.

'Meanwhile Tesco Estates engaged their top team to progress purchase of the station and I met with their leader on several occasions. He seemed respectful of the fight I was putting up but pointed out that, although the station was Grade 2 listed, this was not seen as a safeguard or obstacle. He informed me that they had a team who specialised in acquiring such listed buildings and were confident that this proposal would go through. I passed all this information back to the Chief Executive of the Borough who finally admitted that they could do nothing as they had no money. He had led me a merry dance and lost critical time.

'As it happened there was an entrepreneur in the town that I knew quite well. His name was Roland Pitstock, he ran a property construction company and had been very helpful to the railway while I was in the chair. His father in law had been a fireman at Welshpool for many years and he had often provided us with plant and materials at the weekends at no charge. He and I had always had a good relationship and so I made an appointment to see him.

His office was in the company boardroom – very grand and impressive. His secretary showed me in and he immediately asked, "What do you want now Rowie?" I said that I had a most strange request to which he said that I always had strange requests. I asked him to buy the station building and hang on to it until such time that the railway could purchase it from him. "What do I want with a station?" he asked.

'I told him that the building dated from 1866, that it was the headquarters of the Cambrian Railways and that it would be the "jewel in the crown" of our heritage line. I told him that Tesco had offered £75,000 for the site and that time was not on our side. In the meantime, two high profile hearings were organised which, fortunately for us, dragged on for months. As a result of this delay, I had a call from Tesco one day asking me to meet them. To my surprise they told me that they had lost patience with the process and were withdrawing their offer of purchase. I appreciated that they bothered to tell me personally but couldn't contain my elation! I met my entrepreneur friend again and stressed that he was the only man who could save the station. He said he had a board meeting the next day and would put the issue on the agenda; he promised to call me with the outcome.

'The next day came with no news. Late in the afternoon I rang his secretary again and asked if he was in. "I'll see if he'll speak to you" she said. He came on the phone and said that he should be taken off with the men in white coats to have his head examined – the company had decided to buy the station! I was so overjoyed and relieved to think that the building would be saved for the town and a future railway to enjoy and use. He added that this station had cost him a lot of money, but I told him not to worry – he would get it back. Clearly, he did worry! However, there was a happy ending; not only did he get his money back, but he also won a contract for the station renovation. More importantly the building remains to this day looking ever more majestic thanks to our conversations and his fantastic help. I think it is true to state that our railway is the only heritage line in the country that retains its original headquarters.'

The restored Oswestry South Signal Box, 9 February 2018.
(Paul Carpenter)

The rebuilding of Oswestry station, 9 February 2018. (Paul Carpenter)

The Gas Works Bridge carrying the main road into Oswestry undergoing strengthening by the County Council to allow trains to proceed underneath to Western Wharf, 9 February 2018. (Paul Carpenter)

WELSH RAILWAYS – THE BIGGER PICTURE

Wales is very fortunate in that much of its unique railway infrastructure has either been preserved or is being recreated. This is probably truer here than any other country. The Cambrian line meanders westwards across Wales before diverging north and south along the coast of Cardigan Bay. Its original and primary purpose was to allow people to go about their business, travelling to work, visiting friends or moving freight, etc. It still provides these basic services today, but additionally, it offers wonderful access for tourists to the landscape. The Cambrian line is recognised as one of the most beautifully scenic routes in the country. Passing through the Cambrian Mountains at Talerdigg reveals a cutting that is an extraordinary feat of civil engineering – in the 1860s this was the deepest rock cutting in the world. The sparse open plains of Dovey Junction quickly follow and provide scenes that have remained unchanged for centuries. The journey north up the coast line to Pwllheli is both spectacular and beautiful. The history of the line has been described earlier, but this can be brought alive and experienced today by simply taking this train journey. In exploring the Cambrian lines and adjacent areas, you will have access to several preserved railways.

At Oswestry, rapid progress is now being made with the reinstatement of infrastructure around the headquarters of the Cambrian Heritage line. The main line link at Gobowen is also progressing well and will, one day, again provide Oswestry with a connection to the national system once the A5 road is crossed.

Just up the Dee Valley, a 'steamy Cambrian experience' is authentically recreated on the Llangollen Railway, though historically this was always a GWR line. South of Oswestry lies Welshpool and, apart from the stylish station building, there is the Welshpool and Llanfair narrow-gauge railway. This line was preserved against all the odds and continues today doing what it always did – authentic living history!

At Machynlleth, the Corris Railway once met this important main line station to deliver slate and this railway is being reinstated up in the mountains at Corris. It currently carries passengers over a section of the line and is well worth a visit. The Cambrian main line terminates at Aberystwyth where the Vale of Rheidol winds its spectacular way up to Devils Bridge.

Back on the coast line at Towyn, the beautifully restored Talyllyn Railway steams through the Cader Idris Mountains offering a truly magical and delightful journey. This line was found abandoned in the early 1950s and became the first heritage railway in the world. All heritage railways owe much to Tom Rolt who had the passion, drive and vision to bring this railway back to life. Barmouth Junction (Morfa Mawddach) was once the meeting point with the GWR secondary route from Ruabon, through Llangollen, and Bala to Barmouth. The Bala Lake Railway follows this old trackbed for the length of Lake Bala up to the town.

Adjacent to Fairbourne Station is the Fairbourne Railway which offers a journey towards Barmouth Estuary across the flat sand dunes on the banks of the River

Mawddach. Finally, Portmadoc Station provides a connection with both the Welsh Highland Railway and the Festiniog Railway. The relatively new WHR offers stunning views through Snowdonia National Park to Caernarvon. From here, Llanberis is only a short distance away and is the home of the Snowdon Mountain Railway.

The Cambrian line acts as a conduit to nearly all these preserved railways which is a reversal of its original role. Historically all the narrow-gauge lines met the Cambrian to transfer their materials to markets around the world. Today, the Cambrian is bringing tourists to these preserved lines and the railways are all thriving as a result.

BIBLIOGRAPHY

Beeching, Dr. Richard, *The Reshaping of British Railways*, British Railways 1963

Cozens, Lewis, *The Llanfyllin Railway*, 1959

Christiansen, Rex, *The Cambrian Railways – Portrait of a Welsh Railway Network*,
    Ian Allan 1999

Christiansen, Rex & Miller, R.W., *The Cambrian Railways Volume 1: 1852-1888*,
    David & Charles, 1967

Christiansen, Rex & Miller, R.W., *The Cambrian Railways Volume 2: 1889-1968*,
    David & Charles

Gasquoine, C.P., *The Story of the Cambrian*, Woodall, Minshall, Thomas & Co., 1922

Green, C.C., *Cambrian Railways Album*, Ian Allan 1977

Green, C.C., *Cambrian Railways Album – 2*, Ian Allan 1981

Green, C.C., *The Coast Lines of the Cambrian Railways, Volume 1*, Wild Swan Publications, 1993

Green, C.C., *The Coast Lines of the Cambrian Railways, Volume 2*, Wild Swan Publications, 1996

Kennedy, Rex, *Steam on the Cambrian*, Ian Allan, 1990

Kidmer, R.W., *The Cambrian Railways* Oakwood Press

Lloyd, Mike, *Tanat Valley Light Railway*, Wild Swan 1990

Lowe, Derek, *The Cambrian Main Line, Scenes from the Past No. 55*, Book Law Publications, 2013

Maidment, David, *Great Western Moguls and Prairies*, Pen & Sword, 2016

Maidment, David, *Great Western Small-Wheeled Double-Framed 4-4-0s*, Pen & Sword, 2017

Mitchell, Vic & Smith, Keith, *Branch Lines around Oswestry*, Middleton Press, 2009

Rail Delivery Group, *The Socially Enterprising Railway*, May 2016

Rowledge, J.W.P., *GWR Locomotive Allocations*, David & Charles, 1986

Transport for Wales, *Wales and borders*, 2018

Transport for Wales, *Transforming transport – Community Rail Partnerships and Station
    Adoption*, 2018